D0381469

*To all GaveKal employees, and friends, who have worked hard in recent years to bring us where we are today. Thank you*

The opinions expressed in this publication are not necessarily those of the publisher or the institutions for which the contributing authors work. Although care has been taken to ensure the accuracy of the information contained within the publication, the publisher, authors and their employers accept no responsibility for any inaccuracies, errors or omissions howsoever arising whether through negligence or otherwise.

*Copyright © 2007*

# Contents

# Introduction

The foreign exchange markets have always been the place where the governments of the world have felt free to manipulate the markets, without restraint. From fixed exchange rate systems, to dirty floats, to exchange rates manipulated for mercantilist or political reasons, the list is long and the stories seldom end happily (Argentina in 2001, Asia in 1997, UK in 1992…).

The same is happening today, and, as a result, we have a global exchange rate system which is characterized by a curious mixture of freedom and manipulations. Between the two main currencies of the world, the US$ and the Euro, we have a free float, and this is good. But between the dollar and a lot of other currencies, especially in Asia, we have a dirty float, or fixed exchange rates, the goal being to maintain the exchange rate at an abnormally low parity to the dollar.

To make matter worse, some of those countries (especially China and India) have decided to make their currencies inconvertible (no freedom in the capital account, more on that later). This would not matter if these currencies were small and irrelevant, but they are not. And they are less so by the day. This state of affairs leads to profound price, and volume, distortions, some well understood (i.e.: the RMB is undervalued and can only go up) and some not as well understood. It also leads to a number of important questions. Namely:

- What distortions does the intervention of non-market players in the Asian foreign exchange markets engender?

- Are the distortions abating? Or accelerating?

- How long can those distortions last?

- If/when the adjustment comes, what assets will be most at risk?

Of all these questions, the last one is probably the most important. As we never tire of writing, money management is often more about avoiding the assets that implode, and diversifying amongst the rest, than about picking outright winners. And today, we have to admit that we are surprised to see that the assets widely believed to be the most dangerous (US$, equities, real estate…) offer, in our minds, the most attractive shelters should the current system truly "unravel".

Most of the ideas presented in the following pages were written up by Anatole Kaletsky, Charles Gave, Steven Vannelli and Louis-Vincent Gave for GaveKal Research. The initial papers are all available on our website: www.gavekal.com. The ideas were then further refined thanks to the input of numerous clients. Every morning, as we open our email inboxes, we are reminded of how lucky we are to have clients around the world who take the time to exchange ideas with us, and set us straight when we are wrong. Thanks to our clients, every day, we learn something new. And what could be more fun than that?

# The Long Shadow of the 1997 Asian Crisis

It is hard to underestimate the lingering impact that the 1997-98 Asian Crisis has had on Asian policy makers. In 1997, in the space of a few months, the near-entire burgeoning middle-class of numerous countries was wiped out. And (more alarmingly for policy makers), following this disaster, few policymakers got to keep their jobs. In Indonesia, Suharto was toppled. In Malaysia, a power struggle landed the Deputy Prime Minister, Anwar Ibrahim, in jail for six years. In the Philippines, a wild-card former movie-star was elected to the presidency. In Thailand, a telecom billionaire was elected Prime Minister (both would later be ousted unconstitutionally)…

With the Asian Crisis, Asian policy makers basically learnt one lesson: having an overvalued exchange rate, seeing central bank reserves shrink, running current account deficits, having the IMF in town…all these are things that must be avoided at all cost. And if the cost is to maintain an undervalued exchange rate, then so be it.

Today, like five years ago, it is hard to travel around Asia and not feel that the Asian currencies are undeniably the most undervalued in the world. In fact, if there is a bet that 99 out of 100 investors seem willing to make is that, ten years from now, most of the Asian currencies will be higher against both the Euro, and the US$, then they are today. Stating that (for example), the RMB is set to rise next year hardly takes courage: the currency's fundamentals are solid, the valuation (purchasing parity) is attractive and the technicals are impressive…A more relevant question, of course, is "how do I make money out of that rising RMB trend?".

A year ago, a number of investors would have said: "Simple. Buy the Yen as the Japanese Yen, also undervalued, will ride the wave of the Asian, especially Chinese, currency re-valuation". As we know today, this strategy failed miserably. The Yen ended 2006 as one of the worst performing major currencies (-1% against the US$ and-11.1% against the Euro).

And the Yen wasn't the only one to disappoint. The RMB rose +3.3% against the US$ (so not quite making up the premium on the 12 month forward) but fell (-7.2%) against the Euro. The NT$ disappointed yet again by gaining a meager +0.6% against the US$ and the HK$ actually fell –0.3% against the US$ and –10.6% against the Euro (despite a booming domestic asset market, record IPOs and capital inflows and surging domestic growth). A similar lackluster fate befell the Indian Rupee which rose +1.8% against the US$ and fell-8.7% against the Euro, also despite surging capital inflows and a booming domestic market.

Of course, it wasn't all disappointments for the numerous investors willing to bet on the great Asian currency revaluation. After all, the Korean Won rose +8.6% against the US$ (but fell-2.6% against the Euro); the Singapore Dollar gained +8.4%, the Filipino Peso rose +8.5%, the Indonesian Ruppiah rose +9.3% and the Thai Baht gained an impressive +13.5% against the US$ (though a paltry +1.9% against the Euro).

And as the Thai Baht strengthened, the Thai policymakers showed their hand. The market was told all of a sudden (on December 18th 2006) that Thailand would impose capital restrictions on foreign investors. Following the -16% drop in Thai stocks the next day, Thai policy makers felt somewhat compelled to re-consider and pulled most of the measures announced. Nevertheless, the point was made: policymakers would not shy from using even the most of extreme measures to prevent their currencies from rising further than they (the policymakers) felt was reasonable.

Let us stop for a moment on those Thai events of late December and recap what happened.

- The Thai Baht had risen against the US$, but was still trading at a level far below the levels defended by the Thai central bank before the July 1st 1997 devaluation.

- The Thai Baht was nowhere near overvalued on a purchasing parity basis.

- The government intervened to stem the rise of the Baht in a very clumsy manner (so clumsy that a broker friend of ours sent us the following picture with the heading "Thailand Monetary Policy Committee on its way to a meeting").

© Jim Henson Productions, Inc.

- The government, in an embarrassing volte-face, had to fold under the market's pressure.

But why return to this Thailand side-show? Because the Thailand December debacle triggers, we believe, a very important question. Namely: "what will other Asian policy makers learn from Thailand's mistake?". Will they:

- Learn that the markets are not to be messed with and thus stop intervening on the foreign exchange markets?

- See their belief re-enforced that any rise in their currency must be gradual and managed by the government (i.e.: Thailand's problem is that it allowed its currency to "overshoot" and thus had to resort to extreme measures)?

For our readers willing to invest on the premise that the first answer is correct, may we suggest that they get themselves a bike and join the above crew in a new career? Indeed, if anything, it is likely that the whole Thai debacle will have taught Asian policymakers to keep a close watch on currency changes. And, needless to say, this will continue to have a deep impact on global economic activity, and financial markets.

# Following the Money

The sustained undervaluation of any currency typically leads to an abnormally high rate of return on invested capital in the "goods-producing" part of the economy (think how well Toyota does, and how poorly Ford does, when the Yen is weak and the US$ is high). An undervalued currency can thus be viewed as a subsidy to local production. And, more often than not, this subsidy is paid by the local consumer (who can afford to buy less foreign made goods). A sustained undervaluation also leads to massive FDI (foreign direct investments) inflows and, typically, to trade surpluses. Finally, an undervalued currency can be viewed, in other countries, as a subsidy to consumption (in our example above, thanks to a cheaper Yen, Americans can buy more Toyotas…); this subsidy is paid for by local producers (i.e.: Ford). So today, if we are right in our assertion that Asian currencies are undervalued, and are remaining undervalued because of government intervention, then we can say that:

- Production in Asia is being subsidized to the detriment of Asian consumption

- Consumption outside of Asia (especially in the US and Europe) is being subsidized to the detriment of ex-Asian production.

In an "open economy", when a current account surplus appears, two things can usually happen:

- First scenario: The recipients of the surpluses invest these surpluses directly in the country from which the money came (i.e.: condos in Miami, boats in St Tropez, football clubs in England…). If the sums invested are equivalent in size to those created by the surpluses, then there need not be any impact on the exchange rate of either country. In economic parlance, the capital account surplus compensates for the current account deficit, there is no impact on the domestic money supply, no impact on forex reserves, and thus no impact on the exchange rate. Technically, the country with the current account deficit ends up with more goods and fewer assets (of course, the fact that more money is now chasing fewer assets can lead to a serious price increase in those assets…more on that later), while the country with the current account surplus ends up with more assets and fewer goods…

• Second scenario: The current account surpluses stay in the country earning the surpluses. We then typically have a significant rise in the exchange rate and in the money supply of the country enjoying the surpluses. This is then followed by a rise in asset prices. Which leads to a consumer boom. This then triggers higher imports and higher salaries and, after some time, a disappearance of the trade surplus (see Asia 1994-97)…Either way, the local private sector gets the benefit of the extra work that was done to achieve the trade surplus.

But this is not the way the system works today. By manipulating the exchange rates, or, worse yet, maintaining unconvertible currencies and imposing capital controls, the surpluses generated by the private sectors appear in only one place: the local central banks' foreign exchange reserves.

The way this result comes about is simple: either the currency is convertible (i.e.: Singapore, Hong Kong…) and the market participants generating the surpluses realize quite quickly that their domestic currency is undervalued. In that case, they will keep their cash balances in the local currency, expecting one day a devaluation of the overvalued external currencies. They thus dump their foreign cash balances onto the

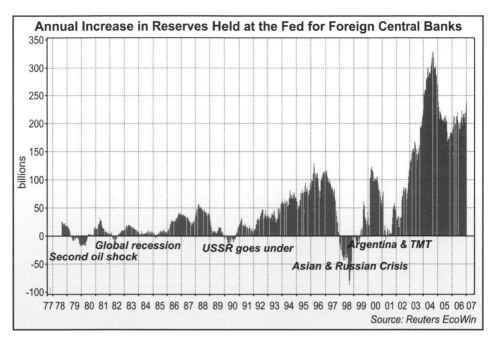

Source: Reuters EcoWin

local central bank. Or the currency is not convertible and the country imposes capital controls, (China, India…), in which case the generators of foreign currency cash have little legal choice but to remit them to the central bank.

Either way, the end result is the same: a massive accumulation of forex reserves in the local central banks.

On the other side of this increase in forex reserves, one would logically expect to see a huge increase in local money supplies. Indeed, when Lenovo turns to the People's Bank of China and says: "here is one million US$, please give me RMB 7.83 million", the PBoC needs to print new RMB before it gets its hands on Lenovo's million dollars and transforms it into reserves. So when central banks intervene to keep their currencies low, hereby accumulating reserves, they usually need to dump their own currencies into the system.

But of course, after dumping their own currencies into the system to prevent them from rising, central banks can turn around and withdraw that money back out of the system. How? By selling some of their local government bond positions to local participants (this is called "sterilizing" the foreign exchange interventions). How does this work? Simple: imagine that you hold RMB 1 million in cash. Tomorrow, the PBoC sells you 1 million worth of bonds. Now you have RMB 1 million in bonds and the PBoC has the 1 million in cash (which it can then destroy).

By sterilizing, the net effect on the domestic money supply will be zero, and nothing happens in the local asset markets or in the foreign exchange market. The local central bank destroys the stimulus coming from the trade sector to the economy, thereby preventing consumption from picking up, and exercising a deflationary influence on the rest of the world. The country with the deficit stays with its deficit (which may, or may not, force the local government to follow a restrictive policy).

Of course, if there is no local bond market of meaningful size (i.e.: China? Taiwan? Hong Kong?...) then the situation becomes more difficult for the central bank. The increase in foreign exchange reserves will end up having an influence on the local money supplies, and the exchange rate. Except of course, if the local central bank uses the currency in which it has surpluses to buy...a third currency, or other assets.

And is this not what is happening today? Asian and oil producing countries on the other side of the US current account deficit are getting US Dollars, but instead of either a) allowing their currency to rise against the US$, or b) buying local bonds to sterilize their FX intervention, they would rather increasingly c) buy other currencies, most notably the Euro (but also the GBP, the AU$, the CA$ and gold...).

Of course, proving this assertion is somewhat problematic since most central banks, for obvious reasons, like to remain opaque as to their currency exposures. But, having said that, the charts below do seem to show that something fishy is happening.

Indeed, when we look at the difference between the Japanese trade surplus, and the amount of assets that the Japanese are buying in the

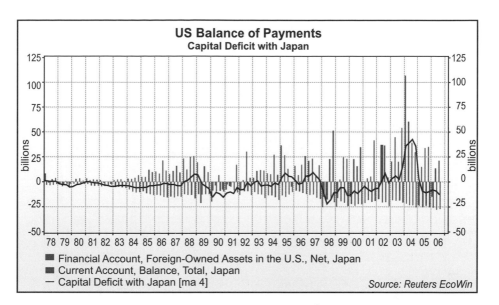

**US Balance of Payments**
Capital Deficit with Japan

- Financial Account, Foreign-Owned Assets in the U.S., Net, Japan
- Current Account, Balance, Total, Japan
- Capital Deficit with Japan [ma 4]

Source: Reuters EcoWin

US, we find that, give or take a few billions, the Japanese are in essence recycling all of the US$ they earn back into the US.

The same, however cannot be said of the rest of Asia. The US exports a lot of dollars to Asia, and few of these make their way back into US assets.

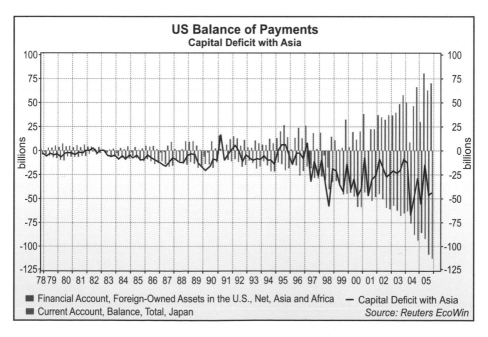

**US Balance of Payments**
Capital Deficit with Asia

- Financial Account, Foreign-Owned Assets in the U.S., Net, Asia and Africa
- Current Account, Balance, Total, Japan
- Capital Deficit with Asia

Source: Reuters EcoWin

So where do these dollars go? It seems that they take a trip to Europe! Indeed, as the chart below illustrates, Europe has recently been buying a lot more US$ assets than its US$ earnings would warrant.

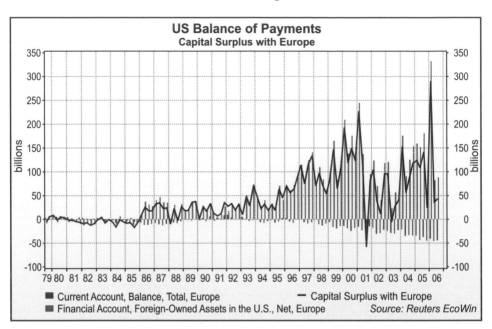

**US Balance of Payments**
**Capital Surplus with Europe**

■ Current Account, Balance, Total, Europe ── Capital Surplus with Europe
■ Financial Account, Foreign-Owned Assets in the U.S., Net, Europe    *Source: Reuters EcoWin*

From there, it is of course one simple step to assume that, as investors, we should just get onto the gravy train that the Asian and oil-producing nations' central banks are driving; simply buy what they buy (Euro, GBP, Gold...). Having said that: everything in financial History teaches us that market manipulations by central banks, and especially systems of fixed exchange rates, can last for a while, but usually end in tears. So how wise is it to continue betting along side the market manipulators? When, and how, will the tide turn?

To try and answer these questions, we must first look at the distortions created by the Asian central banks' currency manipulations.

# Subsidizing Consumption, But What Kind of Consumption?

As stated above, the first net result of the undervaluation of Asian currencies is a net subsidy to consumption outside of Asia.

To a large extent, this big subsidy to consumption has been visible for all to see in the US. Who, by now, has not heard of the over-extended, over-weight, over-leveraged, gluttonous American consumer? But the subsidy seems to have had far less of an impact on the other major global economic sphere, Europe. Or has it?

Frederic Bastiat once said that, in economics, there is always "what you see, and what you don't see". What everyone sees is the amazing fortitude (GaveKal belief) or prodigality (the perma-bear belief) of the US consumer. What few see is that this attitude to spend come hell or high-water is matched across the pond not by the European consumer, but instead by European governments.

Indeed, we would go as far as to say that the structure of consumption is markedly different between the US and Europe. It would be our guess (though note that this is just a guess) that, in the US, 75% of what is described as "consumption" is done directly by the private sector while 25% is done by public entities (government spending, social security etc...). Meanwhile, in most European countries, the ratio is probably closer to 50%-50%.

Why does this distinction matter? Because the two sets of players react to very different factors. The private sector tends to react to prices (i.e.: flat screens TVs get so cheap that everyone buys one) while the public sector tends to react to the ability to borrow without having an undue impact on interest rates. In other words, as long as a politician can borrow and spend, the chances are that he will (witness George W. Bush's impressive expansion in the federal government in his first term).

Another important difference is that the competition coming from an undervalued currency impacts only the private sector. The effects of currency changes on the two groups will be widely divergent.

## Subsidizing Consumption in the US:

When the Asian central banks maintain artificially low exchange rates against the US$, the production of goods in which the US does not have a solid comparative advantage (i.e.: cars?) does not stand a chance. In such goods, we have a structural decline in prices, not always compensated by a rise in volumes.

The decline in the price of such goods leads to a massive increase in the standard of living of most consumers and a rise in real disposable income. This disposable income increase then triggers real estate price increases and increases in service prices. It also leads to the acceleration in the transformation of US companies into platform companies (see our previous book, _Our Brave New World_, for more on platform companies). And, in turn, this has two consequences: an impressive increase in corporate earnings (more on that later), and a simultaneous deterioration in the US trade balance. The two are like two sides of the same coin since, by adopting the platform company model, US corporations are in essence saying "you can take the jobs and the sales; we will take the profits" and, of course, the current account deficit is measured on sales, not profits (more on that later)!

Strong corporate earnings, rising housing and booming domestic consumption then lead to a massive increase in tax receipts. This, in turn, means that, despite George W. Bush's great expansion in federal spending (the largest single expansion since Johnson's "Great Society") the US budget deficit stands at today at below 2% of GDP. As a result, gross US government debt as a percentage of GDP has remained fairly stable (in the 60%-70% range) since 1990:

*Gross Government Debt as a % of GDP*

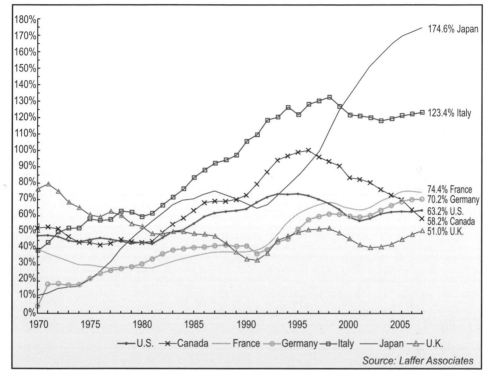

*Source: Laffer Associates*

The same, of course, cannot be said of Europe where government debt has undeniably been on the increase. In both France and Germany, gross government debt as a percentage of GDP has, since 1990, made a serious jump higher (from the 35%-40% range to the 70%-75% range).

## Subsidizing Consumption in Europe:

Milton Friedman famously said that there were three kinds of money: (1) The kind of money that you earn yourself and spend on yourself— this kind, you tend to be very careful with; (2) The kind of money that you earn yourself and spend on someone else—this kind you tend to be a little less careful with; and finally (3) There is the kind of money that you do not earn and that is spent on somebody else—this money, Milton Friedman showed, is never wisely spent.

In the US, the subsidy provided by the Asian government to consumption has been cashed in by the consumer. It has thus been the first kind of "Milton Friedman money". In Europe, the subsidy provided by the Asian currency manipulation has instead, and as the above chart illustrates, been rapaciously grabbed by governments. It has been the third kind of "Milton Friedman money".

Why do governments not spend as wisely as consumers? For a start, the propensity to import of a public consumer is much lower than the propensity to import of an individual consumer (i.e.: public officials would rather use money to buy votes than get the best price for a good or a service). In turn, this leads to a much lower trade deficit, but also a much lower increase in the standard of living, David Ricardo's law of comparative advantages isn't allowed to unleash its full benefits. In turn, this leads to less growth, which then leads to less consumption, itself leading to fewer imports...

If the US consumer was using the Asian subsidy to buy himself a new flat screen TV or a third car, what were the European governments doing with their subsidy? On what did they spend the 30-40% of GDP deterioration in gross government debt? It is of course hard to pin the losses on any one factor. Needless to say, subsidizing a train system which each year loses the equivalent of half of the national education budget (as the SNCF in France regularly does) doesn't help. Neither does the maintenance of expensive social safety nets at times when the unemployment rate seems to remain stubbornly stuck in double digit territory (Germany, France, Italy...). But whatever the culprit is, the result is the same: a very limited growth rate and a constant deterioration of budget deficits.

Some of the European governments, facing declines in tax receipts and increases in debt which push them beyond their European commitments, are facing the situation by raising taxes on the private sector. As such, in 2007, we will witness a VAT hike in Germany and tax hikes in Italy. Meanwhile, the two leading candidates to the French presidency (Mr. Sarkozy and Ms Royal) have both said that they would not "rule out" a "social VAT" to be imposed on goods in order to finance the welfare state.

Poor European producers: already battered by an overvalued exchange rate and poor economic growth, they will also now be facing higher taxes. Higher taxes, high currency and high real rates do not seem to us to be a great remedy for lacklustre growth. European policy-makers should have been officers in the Vietnam War (it "became necessary to destroy the village in order to save it" kind of stuff). Jokes aside, without growth, how is Europe's steadily deteriorating government debt position ever supposed to improve?

# Where Is the Instability?

Let us summarize what we have thus far established:

#1: Asian central banks and policymakers, traumatized by the deep social and political ramifications of the Asian Crisis, have spent the best part of the past decade manipulating their currencies to keep them at an undervalued level. This manipulation is akin to a subsidy for Asian producers and a subsidy to consumption elsewhere.

#2: In the US, the subsidy to consumption has, by and large, been cashed in by the private sector. This has led to a huge trade deficit.

#3: In Europe, the subsidy to consumption has, by and large, been cashed in by the public sector. This has led to an explosion in budget deficits and government debt.

Now is this system sustainable? Our experience of central banks is usually that:

- Central bankers are typically the worst money managers in the World. After all, it is not their money that they are deploying, and they will never be fired for doing a lousy job. To be fair, the simple fact that central bankers cannot take risk almost insures that they will be lousy money managers. They are like boxers with one hand tied behind their backs.

- Central bankers, contrary to popular belief, can be massive agents of instability, giving a false sense of security and competence to the poor guys in the private sector that should know better. In fact they create artificial prices and tell the world that these prices are actual, market-determined prices.

- Most massive misallocations of capital, and the consequent adjustments, can be traced back to the actions of central banks (think Louvre agreement in 1987, Bank of England in 1992, Asia in 1997 etc…).

So, at least based on historical precedents, there are reasons to fear that the current system will prove to be unstable and that the Asian central banks' manipulation of the Asian currency-US$ crosses (which, in turn, has had ripples across a wide array of prices such as other exchange rates, government bonds, risk assets…) could end up blowing up in somebody's face.

But what will blow up? And in whose face?

From the above three points, there are obviously three ways that the current system could implode. Firstly, the Asian central banks could decide to no longer manipulate their currency. Secondly, the US consumer could implode. Thirdly, the European governments could face a crisis.

No prizes for guessing which of the three "possible unwinding" is everyone's favorite. Indeed, going back to the idea that, in economic matters and financial markets there is always "what you see and what you do not see", everyone can see that the US consumer has had a hell of a party in the past fifteen years. And from there, most are willing to accept the idea that the US consumption boom cannot last and that, soon enough, the adjustment will happen through a massive implosion in the US economy.

We disagree. Of the three possible ways that the system rectifies itself, an implosion in US consumption, and in the US economy, actually seems to us the least likely of the three.

# Is the US Current Account Deficit Really Unsustainable?

When we consider global capital flows the really puzzling question is why poor countries such as China or India are saving more than rich ones and why, to add insult to injury, they are lending their money to the rich instead of investing it in their own countries (where presumably they could earn higher returns). This is what our friend Brian Reading has called the mystery of "uphill capital flows". There are, we believe, three explanations to this mystery of "uphill capital flows".

The first explanation is by now familiar to our reader. The "uphill capital flows" are the direct result of simple mercantilist exchange-rate manipulation. As long as China, Taiwan, Malaysia and other Asian developing countries are determined to prevent their currencies from appreciating against the dollar they will intervene in the FX markets, acquiring dollar reserves. Their capital will continue flowing to America regardless of relative returns. Looking at it this way, we could conclude that the US and Asia are part of a single currency zone and in this sense the imbalances between them are no more a problem than the imbalances within the euro zone between Germany and Spain (which incidentally are much bigger than the US-Asian imbalances in relation to GDP). Of course if Asian countries decided to drop out of the dollar zone, they would stop buying dollars. But then their currencies would appreciate, automatically reducing the current account imbalances and therefore the need for capital flows. This would essentially be a self-equilibrating process.

The second explanation is that global growth is moving from developed economies to emerging markets–at its simplest because three billion new capitalists are joining the world trading system. But profits are not migrating to emerging markets nearly as fast as output. The Platform Company effect which we have described in detail in our book _Our Brave New World_ means that more and more production happens in places like China, but profits are still earned in the US and Europe, though possibly booked in Bermuda or the Caymans. When Dell sells a $500 computer in America, this counts as an import from China, but US companies make something like $200 profit, while the Chinese manufacturers would be lucky to keep $50. Because production costs are properly registered in official figures, while profits and value added are not, a large part of the US current account deficit is probably an illusion. In effect, the true imbalances are not $800 billion a year as reported in the statistics, but some much smaller number. This means in turn that the US is not really borrowing $800 billion every year from other countries. This observation is consistent with the fact that the US net foreign debt is today much smaller than the accumulated current account deficits of the past 20 years–in fact the difference is well over one trillion dollars.

The third explanation is that emerging market wealth is accumulating in areas of high political risk and weak property rights. In fact, uncertainty of ownership is probably the biggest risk now facing savers in emerging markets. Add to this the fact that third world capital markets are still somewhat inefficient and emerging market capital will tend to flow naturally to countries with the strongest property rights, greatest political stability and most efficient capital markets. When we ask our clients in Sao Paolo where the top-end property that rich Brazilians like to buy is located, we tend to always get the same answer: Miami. The same is true of bonds with the highest-quality signatures–i.e. US, Germany or Britain, or hedge funds run out of London or New York. In other words, some investors are willing to accept low financial returns in exchange for political stability and secure ownership rights. This preference for high safety rather than high returns is very natural and rational among emerging market investors, the bulk of whose wealth is trapped in business assets located in high-risk/high-return regions.

This phenomenon helps explains another enigma of the US deficits and current accounts: How is it that the US now has a net foreign debt of $2.5 trillion (grey line below), while it still earns a positive net income of almost $30 billion (red line) from these "negative" foreign assets? In other words, the world's "largest debtor" actually runs a positive cash flow on its debt! So much for the unsustainability of the US indebtedness for who ever heard of anyone going bust with a positive cash flow?

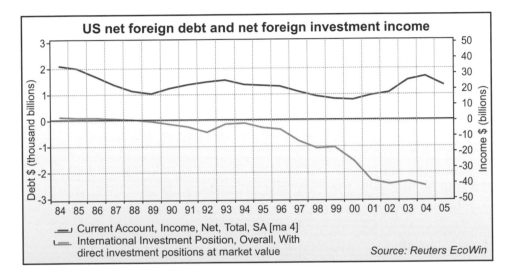

The explanation of this paradox is quite simple: The US earns a much higher rate of return on the assets it owns abroad (roughly 80% of which are either equities or corporate direct investments) than it pays to foreigners on their US assets (which are mostly bonds and bank deposits).

It is often said at this point that the US is behaving like a gigantic hedge fund–with the implication that Americans are running some kind of huge and unquantifiable risks. But the reality is that the US economy is doing something less glamorous. The US is operating simply like a traditional, mundane commercial bank. The bank takes in money from people who are worried about safety and do not have the connections or the skills to invest it, and then invests these deposits in projects with relatively higher rates of return. In return for the safety it offers and for its skill in assessing credit risks, the bank makes a good profit. Incidentally banking has always been a profitable business in every civilization going back to ancient Egypt, China or Mesopotamia. The US today is acting as a banker to the world, especially to the emerging markets and Asia, and is being rewarded for this service (this is even more true, incidentally, of the UK).

To the extent that Middle Eastern investors cannot rely on America to provide them with security of ownership, the shift in global surpluses from Asia to the energy-producing countries helps to explain why the dollar became weaker and the Euro/GBP/CHF stronger as the oil price rose. Note also that this analysis suggests the one truly bearish scenario for the dollar which we can imagine: the big risk to the dollar is not that foreigners will lose their appetite for US assets, but that Americans will refuse to sell any more of their assets to foreigners.

Despite the above facts, almost all economists and policymaking institutions–the Fed, the IMF, the OECD–all absolutely agree on the fact that, even if the US deficits were perfectly harmless or even desirable (and remember that Adam Smith once said *"nothing, however, can be more absurd than this whole doctrine of the balance of trade"*), the US current account deficit would soon have to be narrowed, because borrowing $800 billion a year is simply unsustainable and that today, these deficits present the biggest risk to our system.

But, very immodestly, we believe that all these distinguished experts are exactly wrong.

Indeed, while we cannot be sure whether the present US trade deficits are a good or a bad thing; we have no doubt as to their sustainability. Deficits of US$800bn are perfectly sustainable, not just for many more years and decades but, if necessary, forever. This is a matter of simple and irrefutable arithmetic.

A deficit of $800 billion is a very large number, so we have to put it into some kind of perspective. The standard approach is to compare it with GDP. So we say that America's $800 billion deficit is roughly 7% of its $12 trillion GDP–and this sounds pretty scary because anyone can quickly calculate that 15 years of borrowing at this rate would add up to 100% of GDP. In other words, after 15 years of such deficits, the whole American economy would be in hock. Or would it?

The answer, of course, is a very firm no. The reason is that GDP is not the right factor for scaling the deficits on current account. And even though all economists, the IMF, the OECD… do it, it still does not make it right! Comparing deficits to GDP is simply wrong.

The US current account deficit is a mirror image of a capital inflow, or to put it more emotively, the US trade deficits reflect a country living beyond its means by borrowing from foreigners and selling off national assets.

Let's be even more insulting: America is selling $800 billion worth of family silver every year to finance its shop-aholic addiction (Buffett's share-cropper society). Eventually this rake's progress will surely lead to national bankruptcy, but just when?

To see how long the present rate of borrowing can continue, we should compare the $800 billion America raises each year from pawnbrokers and loan sharks with the total amount of family silver it has left to mortgage, sell or pawn. You may think that this wealth is roughly equal to America's national income of $12 trillion, but you would be completely wrong.

The US is one of the few countries in the world which publishes a detailed balance sheet of national wealth, produced quarterly in the Fed's flow of funds statistics. From this we find that the total assets belonging to the US private sector, net of all government and borrowing, both domestic and foreign, is not $12 trillion but $52 trillion. Gross assets (before netting out household debts and the $2 trillion owed to foreigners) are $64 billion. This figure consists of tangible wealth (mostly housing) worth $26 trillion, equity in quoted companies worth $15 trillion, other financial corporate assets (such as bonds and deposits which also represent part of the net worth of the business sector) of roughly $9 trillion plus $15 trillion of "other" assets, much of it represented by the value of national infrastructure plus the net worth of private non-quoted businesses.

Offset against these $64 trillion gross assets are gross liabilities of $12 trillion, three-quarters of which are accounted by mortgage debts (incidentally the assets and liabilities of the corporate sectors and the US government are cancelled out in these calculations, since the net value of companies ultimately belongs to their shareholders in the household sector, while the financial liabilities of the US government are equal to the government assets held by US households and the overseas sector).

If we accept this official estimate of America's wealth (and we have no reason to discard the Fed's data), the reasonableness of the Fed's figures is suggested by a back of the envelope calculation: suppose there are roughly 100m households in America living and the average house price is roughly $200,000. Then the total gross value of the US housing stock is around $20 trillion, which is very close to the official figure of $19.8 tr.), then our perspective on the current account deficit is completely changed. Instead of saying that the deficit is 7% of GDP or national income, we should say it is roughly 1.2% of US assets. Instead of describing America's net foreign debt of $2.5 trillion as a scary 20% of national income, we can more meaningfully express it as 4% of national net worth.

Much more importantly, America's $52 trillion net worth is not a static figure. Both net and gross wealth in America have been growing by a steady 5-6% in nominal terms every year since 1955. This means that US net worth is growing by roughly $3 trillion each year, while it borrows $800 billion from the rest of the world. So to finance its consumption binge, the US is not exactly scraping together the last of its family silver and sentimental heirlooms; rather it is selling (or more precisely mortgaging) between one quarter and one third of the annual growth in its net worth!

Let us put America's supposed national profligacy into the context of a corporate business. Suppose you were analyzing a company with a turnover of $11 billion, a net worth of $54 billion and $2.5 billion of net debt. And suppose that its shareholders' funds were growing steadily by $3 billion each year. This company comes to you and says that it wants to increase its leverage by borrowing $800m a year. What would you do? You might ask the management whether it had good projects in which to deploy this extra cash. You might ask whether the borrowing program would increase or reduce its long-term RoE. You might wonder whether the company should be even more aggressively or more conservatively managed. But one thing you would not dream of asking is whether this company was about to go bankrupt–remember it is borrowing $800m on the basis of $54 billion net equity and an annual increase of $3 billion in net worth!

You might, however, note that by adding $800m each year to a debt, which begins at only $2.5 billion, the company will be steadily increasing its debt to equity ratio. Given that this debt equity ratio starts at only 4% this would hardly be a worry, but you might, out of pure curiosity, wonder how many years (or decades) the company could keep up this rate of borrowing before the debt-equity ratio started to draw attention from Moody's and S&P. To do this, you would run a spreadsheet which analyzed what would happen to the various financial ratios if the initial rate of borrowing continued for many years ahead.

This is exactly what we can do for the US. Let us start with a debt to asset ratio of 4% and that both GDP and gross wealth grow at a steady 6% per annum. Let us assume that the current account deficit begins at $800 billion and then, far from returning to balance, keeps getting bigger at the same rate as GDP growth (i.e. 6% per annum). The results are summarized in the chart below.

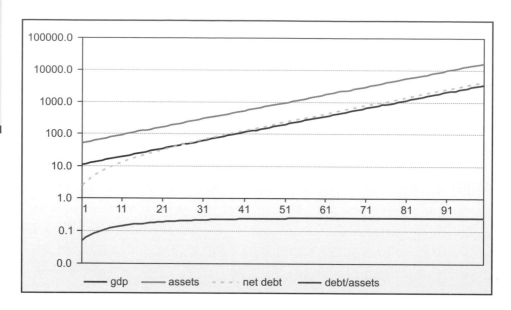

The scale on the left is trillions of dollars–the initial foreign debt is $2.5 trillion, GDP is $11 trillion, US net wealth is $54 trillion and time is shown in years from the starting point. The red line at the bottom shows the ratio of foreign debt to net assets.

What we find is that the US could afford to borrow $800 billion–and continue borrowing this amount, increasing the amount by 6% annually–forever without its foreign debt to asset ratio ever exceeding 26%. In the first few decades of this foreign borrowing program, the debt to asset ratio would rise gradually from an initial 10%, to 13% after 10 years, 19% after 20 years, and 22% after 30 years. After that the growth in the debt equity ratio would gradually tail off, until it stabilized at around 25% after 40 years. By that time, US net foreign debt would be over $100 trillion and the current account deficit would be $8 trillion a year.

These astronomical numbers may sound utterly impossible, but all they really tell us about is the magic of compounding interest, rather than unsustainable profligacy. By 2045, when, on present trends, the US foreign debt would reach $100 trillion, the net wealth of the US private sector would be nearly $500 trillion–and the total wealth of the global economy from which the US would be borrowing would be five to eight times as large.

In other words, even if we assumed that the US deficit, instead of stabilizing or contracting sometime in the future, continues to grow forever at a rate of 6%, there would still be easily enough global wealth to finance this deficit without any problems. The cumulative assets which America would have to sell or mortgage to finance such an ever-expanding deficit would still represent no more than a modest proportion of the country's total net worth.

In saying all this, we do not want to suggest that such a policy of open-ended borrowing would be in America's national interest or optimal from a global standpoint. In principle, we could think of much better alternatives to the present global imbalances.

For example, we would prefer to see a much more expansionary monetary and fiscal policy in Europe. We would also like to see higher exchange rates in Japan, China and the rest of Asia, especially the smaller Asian economies. And we would love to see much lower oil prices, with OPEC producers and Russia forced by WTO rules to offer unlimited production licenses to Exxon, Shell, Total, BP and other Western producers. But none of these blessings seems very likely in the near future. And until this Golden Age dawns, we must return to the question of whether the US current account deficit is unsustainable.

The economist Herb Stein famously observed in the 1960s that if something is unsustainable, then sooner or later it stops. What he meant by this was that if you see something happening in practice for many years on end, then there is no point in arguing that it is impossible as a matter of theory. But strangely enough, most economists these days present this maxim the other way round. They say that deficits of 8% of GDP are obviously unsustainable, and therefore they will have to stop sooner or later. This is simply untrue. For the past 20 years, US trade deficits have been consistently growing, and have consistently been denounced as irresponsible and unsustainable. Yet the same 20 years have seen unprecedented economic stability and accelerating global growth.

Throughout these 20 years the US, Britain, Australia and other deficit countries have consistently shown better economic performance than Japan, Germany, Saudi Arabia and other economies with large surpluses. This experience inspires two opposing conclusions: either you can start from the theory that deficits are unsustainable and harmful and conclude from this that the US or other deficit economies are getting steadily weaker while the global financial system is becoming chronically unstable. Or you can start from the empirical facts-that deficit economies have performed better than ever in the past 20 years and note that the global financial system has been remarkably stable, despite numerous shocks (9/11, Iraq War, Enron, oil at US$70, Katrina, Refco, GM downgrade…). You can then conclude that the theory of unsustainable deficits must simply be wrong.

You have to be awfully confident in your theories to believe that they represent reality, while 20 years of continuous experience is just a fleeting mirage.

# It's Different This Time, or Why Being a Calvinist Doesn't Pay

As previously mentioned, economics is all about "what you see, and what you don't see". Today, everyone can see the increase in consumer leverage, the large gains in asset prices, the record-high corporate profits…and then most people argue that "it can't last". Property prices and corporate profits have to come crashing down. Consumption has to drop dramatically (nowhere more so than in the USA). We are "due" a recession…

But then, there is what too many don't see or refuse to acknowledge. Namely:

- **The Technological Revolution** we are living through is multiplying Man's intellectual strength (just as the first industrial revolution multiplied Man's physical strength). Resources that, until recently, had been locked away in the World's best libraries are now open for all to see; facts and figures which just ten years ago took dozens of hours to gather are now no further than a mouse-click away…Information can be shared almost instantaneously at no cost across any distance.

- **The Financial Revolution** is putting capital within reach of an ever growing number of aspiring entrepreneurs. It is also unlocking wealth from places where, until recently, it laid dormant (real estate, small businesses…).

- **The Healthcare Revolution** allows an ever increasing number of people to live longer, and healthier lives. At the same time, it has started to restrain the rate of population growth in a number of countries, sometimes with dire consequences.

- **The Emergence of Emerging Markets.** Gone are the worries about the next harvest and whether a widespread famine would wipe out the population. Instead, large populations can now aspire to high levels of wealth, consumption and education.

- **Changes in Business Models.** Companies increasingly look to outsource any function in which their value added and returns do not meet certain thresholds; even if that outsourcing takes places across borders, or across continents.

- **A Lifestyle Revolution.** An ever shrinking percentage of total income is spent on essentials (food, clothing…) and a growing share of income is spent on leisure, conspicuous consumption, etc...

Thanks to the above factors, we have witnessed in the past decade a massive drop in the volatility of all economic aggregates. And, in turn, this drop in volatility has had a major positive impact on asset price valuations and the ability of the average consumer to carry debt on his balance sheet. The drop in the volatility of growth is what most people "don't see", yet it is the most important economic development of recent years (so important that it forms the backbone of our previous book, _Our Brave New World_).

These factors explain why, if you take the four biggest Anglo-Saxon economies (USA, UK, Canada and Australia) and look at their growth since 1991, three out of the four have not experienced a recession (and the US recession of 2001 would most likely have been avoided had it not been for the terrorist attacks of 9/11).

This, frankly, is truly remarkable. While recessions, on average, used to occur every six to eight years (the Juglar business cycle), all of a sudden, we seem to have "skipped a beat". Of course, this then raises the question of whether we are due for a massive slowdown? Or whether our economies are undergoing deep transformations which have rendered our economic cycles less volatile than they were in the past? Of course, this does not mean that we will never have a recession ever again, but it might mean that the odds of a recession, (which, as a business owner or a shareholder, should be the biggest fear) are now lower than they were in the past (and thus equity valuations can be higher).

We firmly believe that "things are different this time".

And there is a much more important way that "things are different this time", one highlighted by Alvin & Heidi Toffler in their latest book *Revolutionary Wealth* (a must read). In the book, the Tofflers identify ten characteristics which make knowledge a different input to wealth creation altogether. And as our economies evolve from being industrial economies to being knowledge economies, acknowledging these differences is crucial:

1. Knowledge is inherently non rival: if you use a Microsoft program, it does not mean that there is less for the rest of the world.

2. Knowledge is intangible: We can't touch it or slap it, but we can, and do, manipulate it.

3. Knowledge is non linear. A small breakthrough can lead to huge results.

4. Knowledge is relational. Two apparently separate pieces of knowledge can yield huge results if and when combined.

5. Knowledge mates with other knowledge. Knowledge is very promiscuous and very fertile.

6. Knowledge is more portable than any other product: Once converted to zeros and ones, it can be distributed instantaneously all over the world.

7. Knowledge can be compressed in symbols and abstractions.

8. Knowledge can be stored in smaller and smaller places (including, somewhat to our surprise, Louis' head).

9. Knowledge can be explicit or implicit, expressed or not expressed, shared or tacit. There is no tacit truck.

10. Knowledge is hard to bottle up. It spreads.

Wealth creation today is, for the first time in History, the result of using something which is in unlimited supply, and which has a marginal cost of zero. This puts into question the whole intellectual framework on which the science of economics is built (allocating scarcity rationally). What is the use of marginal analysis when the marginal cost is zero? The core notions on which the markets have been built are changing in front of our very eyes. After all, a market in which the supply is infinite is not a market.

Neither the economists, nor the accountants, nor the analysts have done enough work to understand the implications. What we know is that the tools to measure or manage a knowledge-based economy will be profoundly different than those necessary to measure an industrial based economy. It's simply not about allocating scarcity efficiently anymore.

Proponents of the idea that the past growth rate was borrowed on the future tend to highlight the dumbfounding growth in consumer spending in the US, the "unsustainable" level of consumer debt and the excessive rise in asset prices. The main idea being that both consumers and companies have borrowed excessively to consume today the fruits of tomorrow's labor. This boosted GDP over the short term but, as bills have to be paid at some point, GDP growth is bound to remain below par over the next ten years. Implicit in this argument is a certain "moral judgment", coming either from European socialists or Calvinists: the US has sinned a lot and now needs to pay.

Being neither socialist nor calvinist, we tend to have a more optimistic view of the World. In fact, being catholic, we believe that our sins will be forgiven; being French, we are grateful that they will, since we have a lot to be forgiven for!

# The Chronic US Savings Shortfall

One of the ever recurring claims of the Calvinists is that US inflation numbers are manipulated and bear no resemblance to underlying US economic realities. Meanwhile, we are told, US savings rates and US current account deficit numbers are very relevant and they present a very precise picture of the dire economic condition the US is in.

While we admire this ability to distinguish between "valid" and "invalid" US economic numbers, in our previous book (see _Our Brave New World_), we offer another possible explanation: maybe most of the data points economists like to throw around are becoming increasingly irrelevant? Indeed, today's economic data record changes in "industrial economies"; meanwhile, our economies are increasingly "service/knowledge economies". As such, the US current account deficit is a distraction (see above). And so is the US savings rate.

To illustrate how meaningless a number the US savings rate is, we could of course point out that, for all its lack of savings, the US sports the biggest savings industry in the world; thereby begging the question of "if the US consumer does not save, where does Fidelity, Putnam, Alliance Capital… get their money from? And why, if the US does not save, does the US have the world's biggest capital market?".

We could also point out that the savings rate takes only the income from work and does not include capital gains. It does however deduct from this income all expenses, including expenses to maintain a house and even capital gains taxes! This makes the measure flawed to the point of irrelevancy, especially in a society where capital gains can sometimes outweigh the earnings from work.

The fact that, in 2005, Americans contributed an additional US$650bn to domestic savings products (equity funds, bond funds, etc…) should be enough to discredit the notion that Americans have a "negative" savings rate; as should the fact that American consumers in 2006 had over US$5.3tr in money market funds, CDs, savings accounts and MMDAs, up from US$4.9tr a year before.

But beyond the flaws, and the credibility, of the "US savings rate" which is, despite its obvious failings, so often quoted in the general media, the famous "negative US savings rate" does raise some important questions such as why we save, and how we can possibly measure it.

The answer to that first question is simple enough: we save for a rainy day. And we save for when we get old and can no longer work but still need to consume. After all, as Victor Hugo once said: "*a father can feed ten sons, but ten sons cannot feed a father*".

But what happens if our economies evolve? For example, the economy moves from being agricultural or industrial based and becomes service based instead. Then, as we tried to show in *Our Brave New World*:

a) Rainy days become less frequent

b) We are able to work longer (working at a desk is less demanding on the body then being a steel-worker or an agricultural hand)

This transformation of our economies brings us back once again to Bastiat's "what we see and what we don't see". What we see today, and what all the perma-bears lament, is the collapse in the savings rate. **But what they don't see is that this collapse in the savings rate corresponds to an economic reality:** the fact that our economic cycles are tamer than in the past, the fact that individuals can now manage efficiently (thanks to the financial revolution) both the asset and the liability side of their balance sheets, and the fact that our work is today far less "sweaty" and "dangerous" than it was a generation ago.

In 1985, Franco Modigliani won the Nobel Prize in economics for his work on how companies can optimize the leverage on their balance sheets, depending on the volatility of the economic cycle. Like all good economics, Modigliani's discovery made great intuitive sense: when the economic cycle is tame, companies can borrow more, and vice versa.

Why? Because the problem with leverage is always the fear that, in lean times, one will not be able to make interest payments, and thereby go bust. But if now the 'lean times' aren't quite as lean as they used to be, then the ability to service debt, even at the trough of the economic cycle, is far greater.

And if this is true of companies, why should it be any different for individuals? Given the joint collapse in the volatility of the growth and of employment highlighted in _Our Brave New World_, why shouldn't the consumer borrow more and consume today instead of tomorrow?

Historically, the problem with excessive leverage has always been two fold:

• Rising interest rates (if leverage was underwritten at variable, and not fixed rates).

• The ability to service the debt when one lost his job.

Today, thanks to the emergence of the 'platform company' business model, the likelihood of losing one's job (if one is not an industrial worker) is much smaller than a generation ago. Consequently, the ability to service the debt at the trough of the cycle is less of an issue than it used to be.

When a country moves from agriculture to industry, the volatility of its cycle falls. And, as we argued in *Our Brave New World*, when a country moves from industry to services, the volatility of its growth also falls. And this fall in the volatility of growth has been, we believe one of the most important economic developments of the past two decades.

Not only is this drop in volatility important, it is also very easy to explain. Indeed, if we accept that:

a) services are an ever growing part of the global economy and

b) agriculture is an ever shrinking part of the global economy

Then one cannot escape the conclusion that the volatility of global growth, in both developed and emerging markets, will (barring any major policy mistake) continue to fall. Why? Because there is no worse business than farming, at least when it comes to the visibility of future cash-flows. And there is no better business than services, at least when it comes to maintaining low overheads and low fixed costs. The whole world is going through the transformation highlighted in the diagram below, and this is great news:

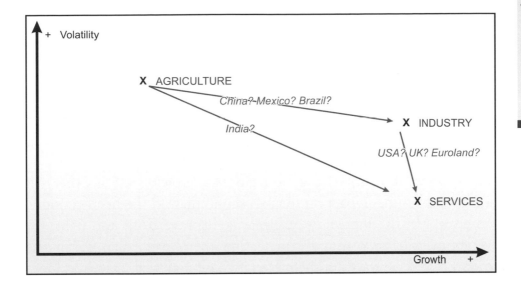

Interestingly, if global growth is now less volatile, then, de facto, we need to save less. And, in turn, this should have an impact on monetary policy. Indeed, if I am working in an environment of rising economic volatility, in which my job is constantly at risk and my prospects of finding a new job are uncertain at best, then I will keep increasing my cash balances. If, on the other hand, like Segolène Royal and her 'partner', I accumulate several civil servant jobs so that my annual combined income reaches over Euros 700,000, then I will no longer have to depend on the whims of clients to get money in my pocket. I will have no reason whatsoever to keep any significant cash balance, and I will go out and buy (and drink) all the fine wines I dare not buy today. To speak like an Austrian economist, in the first case my preference for liquidity will be very high and rising. In the second case, my preference for liquidity will be very low and falling...

And what is true for me is certainly true for the economy as a whole. So beyond the individual consumer's balance sheet, the collapse in the volatility of economic growth should have an impact on broader economic aggregates. And from there, we should probably ponder what that means for policy makers.

Let us take two economies each growing at 3% per year on average.

- The first one (the US from 1964 to 1984) grows at 3% with a high and rising volatility in its quarter-to-quarter growth rate.

- The second one (the US since 1984), is still growing at 3% per year, but this time the quarterly volatility of its output has been divided by three.

It then comes to reason that a monetary base growing at 5% a year will not have the same impact on the two economies. In the first economy, 5% growth in the monetary base may well prove to be too tight, for everybody will be constantly increasing their cash balances. In the second case, 5% growth in the monetary base may well prove too loose as money will be coming out of the woodwork. **This means that looking at money supply growth alone gives a totally incomplete picture of the underlying liquidity environment. Money supply growth needs to be adjusted for the volatility of the underlying economy.**

This is what we try to do in the chart below. The black line is the ratio between the US monetary base and US GDP, base 100 in 1986. The red line on the top graph is the same ratio divided by the quarterly volatility of US GDP. The red line at the bottom is the 2- year rate of change of the second ratio. This is an attempt to measure the liquidity, adjusted for the fall in the volatility of the US economy. And it shows one thing: we

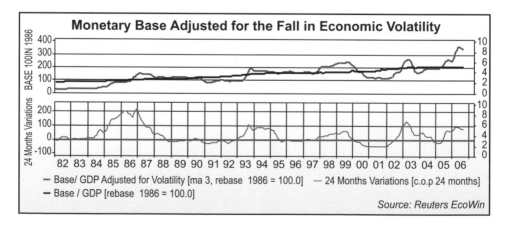

**Monetary Base Adjusted for the Fall in Economic Volatility**

— Base/ GDP Adjusted for Volatility [ma 3, rebase 1986 = 100.0]    — 24 Months Variations [c.o.p 24 months]
— Base / GDP [rebase 1986 = 100.0]

*Source: Reuters EcoWin*

should not worry about running out of cash anytime soon. And if we are not running out of cash, why should we expect people to save?

But there is more to the "lack of savings" story than miscalculations and a change in overall economic environment. We are also most likely witnessing a change in the way people save. To illustrate this, let us imagine a society called "USA-1980" in which most employees work for a big, often industrial, company (Ford, or IBM, Dupont or Chemical Bank). Measuring the savings of all these employees is easy enough: one counts the contribution to pension plans, purchases of savings products…Let us now imagine another society called "USA-2007" in which the big, industrial companies still exist, but they hardly employ the majority of employees. Instead, an increasing number of people work for "sole proprietorship" companies, or for small companies. Even more importantly, today, as opposed to a generation ago, the "most creative" workers will tend to work for themselves, rather than in a big group. Why? Because doing so today is much easier than it was a few decades ago (easier technology, lower set-up costs, lower admin costs…).

This is not hypothetical: the number of S-corps filings in the US more than doubled over the 1980s, and by 1995 S-corps made approximately half of all corporate filings. In 2003 there were 3,444,400 S-corps that filed a tax return with the IRS. This number is up 4.8% from 2002 and up 354% from 1985.

Now why would the differences in the nature of the employer matter? Speaking from personal experience, it makes a world of difference.

For a start, when one works for a big company, one could be fired at any time, so one needs to "save for a rainy day". When one works for one's self, one is less likely to be fired…though times, of course, can be lean.

Which brings us to the second very important point: when one works for one's self, the natural reaction is to plow back all of one's excess income into one's business (again, speaking from experience!). In essence, the savings is done through the business; and these savings are simply not captured by national accounts.

This last point brings us to a fascinating paper written by the Minneapolis Fed (http://minneapolisfed.org/research/WP/WP636.pdf) entitled *Expensed and Sweat Equity*. In the paper, the authors (McGrattan and Prescott) explain that GDP, as it is calculated today, is massively distorted by the fact that *"Expensed investments are expenditures financed by the owners of capital that increase future profits but, by national accounting rules, are treated as an operating expense rather than as a capital expenditure. Sweat investment is financed by worker-owners who allocate time to their business and receive compensation at less than their market rate. Such investments are made with the expectation of realizing capital gains when the business goes public or is sold. But these investments are not included in GDP. Taking into account hours spent building equity while ignoring the output introduces an error in measured productivity and distorts the picture of what is happening in the economy…We find that expensed plus sweat investment was large during the recent boom... and critical for understanding the dramatic rise in hours and the modest growth in measured productivity."*

This notion of sweat equity is of course very appealing to anyone who has gone through the initial tough years of building a business (again, speaking from experience). And it makes perfect sense. Take our own business as an example: GaveKal today, a Hong Kong registered company, is worth, on paper, HK$10,000… But none of the partners (who own the business outright) would be too keen to sell any of their shares at that price. Why, because we have so much "sweat-equity" invested in the business. And of course, the same goes for any small business owner.

For most small business owners, valuing the "sweat equity" is a challenging task. Moreover, the "sweat equity" represents most small business owners' net worths…In other words, their savings, though these savings appear nowhere in national accounts.

This means that the fall in the savings rate in the US over the past twenty years could partially be a reflection of the fact that a very large number of

Americans have moved from being employees, to being entrepreneurs. And if so, why should we bemoan that trend? And what is unsustainable about it?

In his book *Running Money*, Andy Kessler likes to say (referring to the US current account deficit), "we think, they sweat". That is not far off the argument we ourselves made in 2004 in our little booklet *What Investors Should Know About the US Current Account Deficit*. But having said that, and according to the researchers at the Minneapolis Fed, Americans think, and then they sweat! Quoting from their paper: "*Our estimate of intangible (expensed plus sweat) investment in the business sector is a little over 3% of GDP during the 1990s, rising to over 8% of GDP at the peak of the boom in 2000*". These are huge numbers: that's US$300bn to US$800bn! Especially when put in comparison with the annual US$7tr in wages and salaries. Adding the "sweat equity" to the savings rate would thus boost the savings rate by 4.2% to 11.4%... i.e.: no more negative savings rate.

And frankly, this makes perfect sense to us. For everywhere we care to look, we see sweat equity at work. Think about Vietnamese immigrants opening a dry cleaners in which the whole family works. Think about computer engineering students that get together to form the next Google. Think about a bunch of young musicians who work together for years to get a contract. Think about a hedge fund. Think about a guy who likes to restore classic cars…And then, of course, there is the elephant in the room: the young couple that buys a fixer-upper and pours its savings into its home (again, speaking from experience…).

According to the 2000 census, there were 116m housing units in the US. Assuming a 10% growth since then (the US has had an important construction boom and an increase in population), we would guess that there must be around 125m-130m homes in the US today. That is a lot of places for people to deploy "sweat equity".

One of the ways one knows that Americans have been pouring sweat equity into their residences is by looking at the growth in sales of Home Depot or Loews. Today, it feels as if one cannot drive through a 20,000 person town in America without seeing at least one, if not several, home improvement stores. Clearly, there is a market for the lumber, tiles, and lighting fixtures that they sell.

So let us return to the young couple that buys a fixer-upper. The purchases made at Home Depot are accounted as an expense (and not depreciated over time but completely front-loaded instead). The time they spend improving their home appears nowhere in national statistics. Until, of course, they end up selling the house at which time they will register a capital gain. But that capital gain is not included in our couple's savings rate. And, if they have a capital gain tax to settle (maybe it is a second home…), the tax payment will be deducted from the revenue they get from work and they will thus show a negative savings rate!

This example on housing also brings us to a side-point: for almost all Americans, the purchase of a house is by far the biggest purchase they will ever make and constitutes around 80% of their lifetime savings. This means that a savings rate that does not include what happens in housing completely misses the boat. It ends up being massively skewed towards the higher income segment of the population.

In essence, the savings rate is as skewed as the tax burden, whereas 20% of the people pay 80% of the tax, we would guess that 20% of the people in the US probably account for 80% of the so-called savings rate. And these 20% of people are ever more mindful of finding places for their savings away from the government's eyes; and they have the means to do so.

Given the expansion in the balance sheet in the American household, and the rude health of the US savings industry (Alliance Capital, Vanguard, Fidelity…don't seem to be complaining of a "dearth of savings"), it stands to reason that capital from somewhere is pouring in. We do not expect companies to grow retained earnings or book value without earning any money. So we probably should not expect it of the US consumer either.

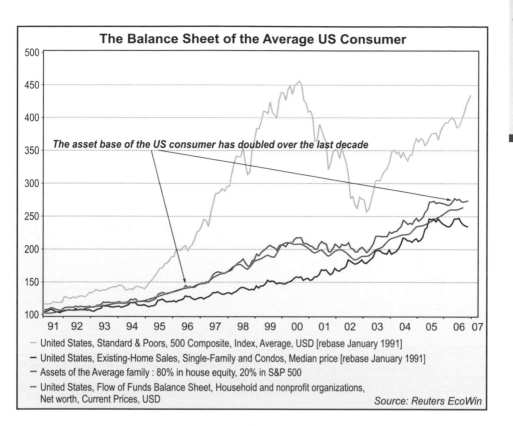

**The Balance Sheet of the Average US Consumer**

*The asset base of the US consumer has doubled over the last decade*

— United States, Standard & Poors, 500 Composite, Index, Average, USD [rebase January 1991]
— United States, Existing-Home Sales, Single-Family and Condos, Median price [rebase January 1991]
— Assets of the Average family : 80% in house equity, 20% in S&P 500
— United States, Flow of Funds Balance Sheet, Household and nonprofit organizations,
   Net worth, Current Prices, USD

*Source: Reuters EcoWin*

Most Calvinists would answer that the US consumer has grown his balance sheet through leverage, financed by foreigners. This, of course, is true. But it is not a complete explanation. There has to be some other form of "unreported savings" that flow into the balance sheet expansion. Indeed, US households net worth will grow between US$3-4 trillion this year (see previous chapter), on the back of less than US$800bn in foreign capital. This doesn't seem to add up. There must be more domestic capital being employed than the reported statistics would have us believe.

Housing has been the asset that has really carried the balance sheet expansion of the last few years. But if people "invested" increasing sweat equity in their business while stock prices rose in the 1990s, are they "investing" increasing sweat equity in their homes today? Maybe, just maybe, US asset values, in aggregate, rise year in and year out (though different assets) on a more balanced path? Maybe it isn't just explosive debt growth, as most perma-bears argue, but a healthy level of savings mated with appropriate levels of debt that cause asset values to consistently rise?

And maybe, just maybe, the system will prove to be as sustainable over the next twenty years as it has been for the past twenty?

# The Importance of the Stock of Savings in Determining the Cycle

In this book, we have argued that the drop in the volatility of economic growth has been one of the most important economic developments of the past few years. This fall in volatility has allowed entrepreneurs to project themselves further into the future, consumers to borrow more, etc...

And of course, success has many fathers, so one can find many explanations behind the fall in the volatility of economic growth: globalisation, lower inflation, etc... Another factor could well be the rise in asset prices (triggering the old question of the chicken and the egg, or which came first: the drop in the volatility of growth or the rise in asset prices). Let us explain.

Most people, when they spend money, look at three things:

- How much money are they making (i.e.: salarics + bonuses)

- What is the value of their assets and

- What has been the performance of these assets over the last few years

Consumption is certainly not a function of the first factor only (which incidentally, is why the US savings rate is meaningless since it simply takes the difference between annual spending–including capital gains taxes- and annual salary, without even adding capital gains!). **For an economist, there should be no difference between income and capital gains.**

This is all the more true since the savings picture can be distorted by tax policies. For example, since increases in income tend to be taxed at the highest marginal tax rates, and capital gains at lower rates, it stands to reason that anyone who can influence how his income is to be distributed will choose the capital gain route. An economy with a growing number of entrepreneurs (such as the US) will de facto record a falling savings rate, and this despite the fact that the higher your "income", the higher your propensity to save. Rich entrepreneurs will simply pick the "capital gain solution".

If our reader accepts what we just wrote, then the question immediately becomes: how do we reintroduce the "capital gains" in the "income" to have an idea of how much individuals are really making, and saving. This is what we try to do in the chart below; to the officially declared "income", we add the increase over the previous five years of the assets held by the US individuals, net of all debt.

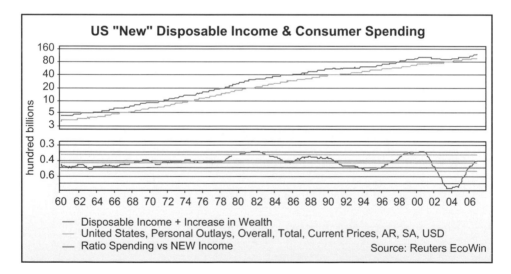

Our logic is simple: an increase in the value of an asset over the previous five years is probably solid enough to be incorporated in one's mind as being for real, and can thus be used to increase one's spending. The results are quite interesting: our ratio (contrarily to the classical savings ratio) always returns to the mean. When there is a recession, the US consumer will not mind using his assets to "smooth" his consumption. Similarly, when there is a boom in asset prices, and contrary to popular belief, he will let his true "savings rate" go up tremendously.

When recessions are preceded by periods of five years without asset price increases (1974, 1982), recessions tend to be very severe. Recessions preceded by significant increases in asset prices tend to be much milder (2001). Contrary to what our perma-bear friends might argue, **rising assets prices are thus a stabiliser for future economic activity. And with this in mind, given the recent boom in asset prices, proponents of the belief that we are on the verge of a brutal meltdown in US consumption will most likely be disappointed.**

At this stage, our reader may wonder how the GaveKal Savings number for the US compares with the official savings rates (now negative) as provided by the BEA. This is the chart below.

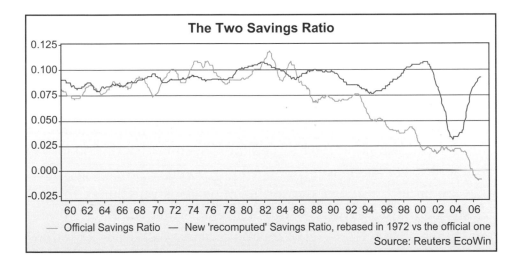

Interestingly, up to 1986, there was very little difference between the two savings ratios. Since 1987, however, the two time series have started to diverge significantly, a fact which leads us to wonder whether the decline in the official savings ratio (which started in 1986) isn't just a function of the bull market which started in 1982?

For the sake of argument, let us imagine a world with only two countries, one in which asset prices are going up structurally, and one where asset prices are going down structurally. The country with falling asset prices will exhibit a total absence of increase in consumer spending. In such a world, the unhappy country will have a current account surplus, and the happy one a deficit. This will simply mean that the unhappy country is badly managed, and the happy one well managed.

If we apply this model to the relationship between the US and Japan, we all know that Japan has enjoyed very little asset price appreciation in the past fifteen years. The lack of asset price appreciation forced the Japanese to save a lot, pushed them into massive trade surpluses, and engendered constant capital outflows from Japan as investors hunted returns around the World. If the American authorities had followed a policy to prevent the Japanese (and the Asians after 1997) from rebuilding their asset base (as Mr Hoover did in 1932), we would most likely have had a global depression. Through its current account deficit, the US provided some kind of a Marshall plan to Asia (and it was badly needed).

The good news today is that most Japanese companies and individuals, along with other Asian countries, have rebuilt their asset base (and then some!). We should thus start to see a massive fall in the "official" savings ratio in Asia, i.e. a consumer boom of unheard proportions. As our more faithful readers know, we have argued for some time that this boom will take the shape of an infrastructure spending boom in ASEAN and a real estate boom in China (see our forthcoming book on China). In turn, this should lead to a collapse in the current account surpluses all over Asia, and a much higher level of economic activity all over the world.

In today's world, investing in a country with a current account surplus (Japan, Germany, Switzerland...) more often than not means investing in a low-growth, poorly managed economy. Meanwhile, investing in countries with large current account deficits (Australia, Spain, US, UK...) has not led to financial ruin. Current account surpluses are not profit and losses statements, but simply the reverse of the capital account. A well managed country will tend to have a capital account surplus, and thus will have a current account deficit. Using current account deficits as an investment yard-stick makes no sense whatsoever.

# Does Comparing Savings Rates Across Countries Make Sense?

Beyond bemoaning the unsustainability of the US current account deficit, and the dearth of US savings, another favorite lament of market participants inclined to believe that the instability of the system will be resolved through an implosion in US consumption is to compare the US savings rate with the savings rate of other nations. From there, it is but one step to the conclusion that, because the US has a low savings rate, the US will be unable to invest in its future and will thus suffer lower productivity gains, lower growth than other regions around the world, etc…

Of course, the fact that nothing of the sort has happened in the past twenty years, and that, in recent years, both economic growth and productivity gains in the US have been very impressive (even despite the negative savings rate) does not shake the belief of those who maintain that the lack of US savings will erode the US' position in the world.

The US savings rate is a deeply flawed and irrelevant measure. And taking that measure to compare it to other savings rate around the world strikes us a particularly meaningless exercise which offers precious little insight. After all, the fact that China has a high savings rate may simply reflect that: a) nearly half of its population still works in the fields (and thus need to save a lot of their earnings in the fear that, come the next harvest, rain will be either lacking or too abundant), b) China has no social safety net to speak of and an insurance industry still in its infancy (thus if you are injured at work, you best have a lot of savings to tie you through until you get better), and c) a different demographic structure than the US.

On this last point, we would like to ask our reader a few simple questions.

Q1: Who, in the OECD, has the worst savings rate?
Answer (for our readers who have just landed from Mars): the US

Q2: Who, in the OECD, has the highest savings' rate?
Answer: Japan, Italy and Germany...

Q3: Who, in the OECD, has the best demographic trends?
Answer: the US

Q4: Who, in the OECD, has the worst demographic trends?
Answer: Japan, Italy, Germany...

Is the fact that the highest savers in the world also have the worst demographics a pure co-incidence? We do not think so, for the following reasons:

- Firstly, kids, as all new young parents quickly find out, cost money. A lot of it. And everyday a little more (e.g.: education costs have steadily been rising faster than inflation for the past two decades). So if nothing else, we should expect people that do not have kids to save more than people who do.

- Secondly, at different ages, people present very different consumption patterns. Young people (and societies) tend to consume a lot of goods (TVs, cars, ovens...). Meanwhile older people tend to consume services (opera tickets, cruises, hip replacements...). In countries such as Japan, Germany etc...the "expensive services" (namely healthcare) are delivered by a government monopoly. So what can old people do with their money except save it? Aside from Charles, most old geezers are not buying flat screens or iPods.

Staying with the above idea, in most Western economies, the social benefits (pensions, healthcare…) on which old people rely are typically dependent on a growing population. Today's young pay for today's old in an intra-generational show of solidarity. But what happens when the young people fail to show up? Who then pays for the old people? This is not a moot point: in Japan, Germany and Italy, the populations have started to shrink. So one might think that people in these countries are right to save; for if they plan to rely on the payments' from young people to see them through their old age, they will be mightily disappointed.

Given a) how most of our welfare states have been organized, and b) the rapidly deteriorating demographic situation, people in the countries with ageing and shrinking populations need to save if they want to ensure a decent standard of living for themselves since the state may well end up being unable to provide it.

Finally, and just as importantly, having kids has historically always been a guarantee for one's old age. Indeed, people often had kids to ensure that when they grew old, they would be taken care of (this, at least, has been Charles' strategy and, so far, it seems to be working…). In other words, when you have kids, you don't need to save as much since you have a "moral claim" on a small part of your children's future earnings.

The irony, as a client recently put it to us, is of course that, in today's rich Western societies, we are now "too poor to have kids", or at least, too poor to have a lot of them. Consequently, the world is dividing up between aging, rich, societies with high savings rate and young, expanding societies with low savings rate. Is that low savings rate a problem? To whom does the future belong? The high savings societies that produce no kids? Or the "spendthrift" societies that invest in their youth?

As Jean Bodin once said: "il n'est de richesses que d'hommes" (the only wealth is man).

# CHAPTER 10

# An Odd Phenomenon

At the beginning of this book, we made the assertion that the Asian policymakers' decision to manipulate their currencies into undervaluation ended up creating a subsidy for US consumers and Asian producers. We also argued that this subsidy was paid for by US producers and Asian consumers.

However, looking at the chart below, it would be hard to argue that US companies have suffered unduly from "paying" this subsidy. As we write, gross after tax cash flow margins are making record highs (and, despite a popular and widely held belief, show no "mean-reverting" tendency whatsoever).

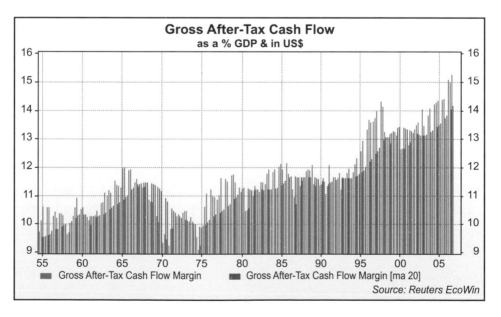

How can this be? How can US corporations be earning ever more money in the face of what should be an "overvalued US$" (at least, if the US current account deficit numbers are to be trusted)? How are US companies able to maintain their profitability despite Asia's cut-throat competition?

Just like success has many fathers, there are, we believe, several explanations to the impressive profitability of US corporations.

The first is simple enough: thanks to the Reagan supply-side revolution, and thanks to the Bush tax cuts, the government takes less out of the company's pockets than it used to. This leaves more for shareholders.

The second explanation is also easy enough to understand: thank to the collapse in inflation, and the collapse in interest rates, companies today spend a lot less money servicing their debt than a decade ago. And what they no longer have to pay their bankers ends up in the pockets of shareholders.

The third, and possibly most important, explanation is that US, and other western corporations are evolving from being industrial, low margin producers, to being high margin service providers. As OECD economies transform themselves from industrial economies to knowledge economies, the value companies add rises (for more on that topic, see chapter 22).

The fourth, and final, explanation for the impressive expansion in profit margins is of course, globalization.

In most western countries with ever-growing shareholder activism and ever-improving management techniques, an increasing number of companies have become parsimonious with their capital spending. Capital is only deployed on projects which are deemed to bring returns over a certain threshold. Functions in which the company does not add value are either shut down, or spun off and sold to other investors better able to generate value. In the western world, what matters first is profits and returns on invested capital. Employment then comes as a natural consequence of the companies' profit seeking activities.

But in a country like China, things are very different. Thanks to a low cost of capital and a very low cost of labor, companies have sprung up all around the country and piled into new businesses. And because returns on invested capital are a distant consideration, most sectors are in overcapacity; and yet capital spending continues regardless. The country thus has over 300 auto producers, 3,000 ball bearing manufacturers… In China, what matters first and foremost is employment; profits are a secondary consideration at best.

The US and China could of course each live as islands unto themselves (and if Chuck Schumer had his way, that is probably what would happen). But fortunately, the past twenty years have been characterized by ever greater improvements in communication technologies, port infrastructure, airplanes…Encouragingly, trade barriers and impediments to the movements of goods, and people, have been rapidly collapsing. As a result, we live in a world in which China and the US can increasingly talk to each other. And when they do talk, what do they say? China says "all I want is jobs" and the USA says "all I want is profits". And in that discussion a deal can rapidly be struck.

Is it a coincidence that, just as we saw a widening of the US current account deficit, we also witnessed an explosion in the profitability of US corporations? Readers of *Our Brave New World* will hopefully answer "no".

Would it be a stretch to say that the impressive, and unprecedented, growth in US profits of the past few years is directly linked to Chinese companies' inability to hold on to any recurrent profitability? As the trade between the two economic giants keeps on growing, one question that investors should ask themselves is "who captures the bulk of the profitability of the trade flows?" Is it Wal-Mart (or some other US distributor)? Or is it the Chinese goods manufacturer?

# CHAPTER 11

# Opening Up a Can of Worms

This new world order through which rich nations get the profits and poor nations get the jobs immediately creates an immediate quandary, namely massive income disparity.

In the "pre-Brave New World days", people sitting at the bottom of the socioeconomic ladder could get well-paid manufacturing jobs and ensure decent living standards for themselves and their families. The

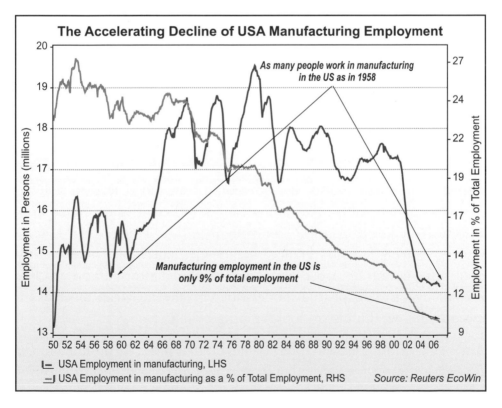

**The Accelerating Decline of USA Manufacturing Employment**

As many people work in manufacturing in the US as in 1958

Manufacturing employment in the US is only 9% of total employment

└── USA Employment in manufacturing, LHS
─┘ USA Employment in manufacturing as a % of Total Employment, RHS   *Source: Reuters EcoWin*

problem today is that, as the US-China trade of "we take the profits and you take the jobs" gets made, the people who were previously holding those jobs could be seen as losing out. If nothing else, the "well paid" manufacturing jobs are disappearing at a record pace (again, the "what you can see" component of the current economic transformation).

As the title of this chapter suggests, the trade currently in place whereby "we take the profits, they take the jobs" (which, looking at both the profit data, and the industrial job numbers, seems to be well in place) opens up a massive can of worms. Indeed, if nothing else, industrial jobs tend to be fairly well distributed within a population; most people have the skills to obtain, and maintain, an industrial job. Unfortunately, the same cannot be said of profits; profits tend to be concentrated in the hands of a society's richest members (the shareholders).

So as we trade industrial jobs for higher corporate profits, we also witness growing income disparity across much of the Western World.

Let us be clear here: in recent years, the poor have not gotten poorer… but the rich have definitely gotten much wealthier. According to Fed's flow of fund figures, in the early 1970s, the income share of the top 1% of earners was less than 10% of total income. Today, it stands at 20%. This means that the top 1 million households in the US earn on average US$1.8m each. That is more than twice (adjusted for inflation) what the top 1 million households were earning thirty years ago.

This growing income disparity, one could fear, might lead to political problems and tensions. Are our societies sufficiently mature to cope with such income disparities? Some might be (US? Hong Kong? UK?...). Others, maybe less so (France? Italy? Germany?...). There is little doubt that countries seeped in Marxist thinking and tradition will find it challenging to adapt to a model whereby the rich reap most of the rewards, and wealth disparities keep on growing.

And yet, economic growth today comes, at that price. As outlined in _Our Brave New World_, we can either accept income disparities, or slip into economic irrelevance.

# Learning to Accept Income Disparity

In <u>*Our Brave New World*</u>, we tried to show that economic growth was typically triggered either by an efficient reorganization of talents (we called this Ricardian growth) or by new inventions (we called this Schumpeterian growth). We further argued that, while Ricardian growth had limits (you can only rationalize and reorganization a given structure of production so many times until all the inefficiencies are squeezed out), Schumpeterian growth was limitless. Man will always come up with new inventions. So, in some respect, Schumpeterian growth is somewhat more interesting to study than Ricardian growth.

As most of our readers know, Schumpeterian growth can be as destructive as it is creative. This is why Schumpeter called the growth process 'creative destruction'. A quick example: when the fax machine was invented, it spelled the doom of the telex machine (who nowadays has a telex machine in their office?). And when email was invented, the number of faxes sent collapsed…

So how does one promote Schumpeterian growth? We believe that you need at least three very important variables to be in place:

### #1: The Right, and the Ability, to Fail

As mentioned above, one man's invention is often another man's ruin; there is a dark side to the force of capitalism. For decades, this dark side of the force has deeply disturbed governments. Firstly, because the dark side appears inhumane. Secondly, because special interest groups threatened by the dark side can be very organised and vociferous (steel industry in the US, construction industry in Japan, farmers and rail workers in France...), bringing to politicians the two things they need (votes and money). Thirdly, because politicians typically think that they can control, for the greater good, the might of the dark side. Unfortunately, more often than not, attempts to reduce the effects of the dark side only end up stifling the creative side of the force. Rather than protect jobs, protectionism, market regulation, measures and laws that prevent competition typically block future inventions and current growth.

## #2- The Legal Protection of Intellectual Property

In the knowledge economy in which we now live, 'value' is increasingly domiciled in intellectual property. Stripped of intellectual property, what would Microsoft be worth? Or Novartis? Or GaveKal? Okay, that last one is probably a stretch since GaveKal is not worth much...but our reader gets our drift. Without a healthy respect for intellectual property, and established legal procedures to defend it, Schumpeterian growth simply cannot flourish.

Establishing the legal framework in which intellectual property can flourish is not easy. It is also an everyday task given the constant evolutions in _Our Brave New World_; for example, the US Supreme Court recently had to establish the legality, or not, of music file sharing over the Internet.

Today, intellectual property is decently protected in the Western World but it is not in the greater Emerging Markets. This important difference helps explain, we believe, why so many platform companies are domiciled in the Western World, and so few are in the emerging countries.

This stark difference, however, does not mean that all is rosy for the Western economies, and that good ideas and new processes will only continue to emerge from there. Far from it. In fact, one point of serious concern is that politicians all across the Western World are making the mistakes of their forefathers all over again. Let us explain through the British example.

Following WWII, the British Labour party identified three sectors as the 'growth sectors' of the economy: steel, coal and rail. The government then said that these growth sectors would be better managed by the state. Of course, we know what happened. Today, Britain has no steel, coal or rail industry to speak of. The nationalization of these important sectors prevented ideas from flourishing; creative destruction could not apply.

Today, all over Europe, governments are up to the same trick. While they are happy to leave rail, coal and steel by the side (having destroyed these industries), the three new 'growth' sectors of the future have been identified by governments. They are: education, pensions and healthcare. But in a growing number of countries, the governments are saying: these three sectors are the 'chasse-gardée' (protected area) of the government. No-one else is allowed to butt in.

This can only mean two things. Firstly, that capital will be wasted (and because these sectors require increasing amounts of capital, the governments will either take it from the taxpayer, or-more likely- finance it through deficits). Secondly, that the growth of ideas, and the pace of creative destruction, will be unfortunately restrained.

### #3- The Acceptance of Income Disparity

More than the above, Schumpeterian growth also needs an acceptance by society of important income disparities. Indeed, what is the point of working hard and putting together new inventions if a government takes all profits away in the name of social equality? Any country aiming to promote Schumpeterian growth needs to recognize that the desire to strike it rich remains the greatest motivator. In 1982, Deng Xiao Ping announced that 'to get rich is glorious'; since then, China has not looked back and the income of China's city dwellers has increased 14 times.

This acceptance of income disparity is probably the hardest thing to achieve in the current political structure of most countries. Why? Because most countries oppose the 'social' to the 'unequal' and strive to avoid wide income disparities.

But the refusal to accept income disparities is a very destructive act. Inherently, it implies that capital is taken from where it is efficient and generating high returns, and distributed where it isn't. Such a course of action can only lead to an impoverishment of the greater society; and when the greater society gets poorer, it is the poorest members who suffer the most. Time and again, this has been the experience of socialism.

Trying to prevent the growth of income disparities is also denying an important economic reality: income disparities are a tremendously creative force. As Thorstein Veblen showed in *The Theory of the Leisure Class*, one of the main motors of capitalism is the desire for conspicuous consumption; or, as popular knowledge calls it, the wish to 'keep up with the Jones'. If there are no Jones to keep up with, why get out of bed in the morning?

Looking around the world today, we find that the economies riding Alvin Toffler's 'third wave' to the limit of its potential all take a benign view of income disparity, whether the US, the UK, Australia, Hong Kong…

Staying on Hong Kong, the city-state surely ranks as one of the greatest success stories of the past fifty years; and no first time visitor to the city fails to be shocked by:

a) How vibrant, and wealthy, the city is and

b) The disparities of wealth on display

Hong Kong's economy was destroyed by the Japanese in WWII, destroyed by the UN embargo on trade against China in 1951, and crimpled by worries over the return of the territory to China. Hong Kong has been hit by typhoons, mud-slides, squatter-camp fires, bird-flu, SARS and massive refugee influxes. Hong Kong has no mines, no oil wells, and very little agriculture. Hong Kong also has nowhere to park; yet, the town has the highest ratio of Rolls Royce, Ferrari and Porsche per capita.

And Hong Kong also has one of the lowest rates of violent and non-violent crime in the world. How did Hong Kong achieve this success? By encouraging wealth disparity. Hong Kong is a city without minimum wage where the wealthy and enterprising reap huge rewards.

And yet there is little social tension. Why? Because the unfortunate workers at the bottom of the ladder believe that one day, things will be better. This is a very important point: income disparities are untenable when there is no hope of social advancement. But that is not the case in the US, the UK, Australia, Hong Kong where you find lots of rags to riches stories (e.g.: Li Ka Shing). And even more rags to middle class stories.

When the process of creative destruction is allowed to work, we have both income disparity and the ability of people to 'move up'. When income disparity is constrained, the ability of people to climb the social ladder disappears. More than anything, the inability to accept income disparity is, we believe, what ails an otherwise tremendously productive country like France.

# A Serious Political Risk

The fact that, thanks to globalization, outsourcing, and the adoption of the platform company model, US corporate profits keep making record highs should not be bemoaned; it is excellent news, not only for the 60% of Americans who own shares (whether directly or through their pension plans) but for the greater society at large.

Of course, a Marxist would argue that the constant rise of corporate profits as a % of GDP is not a good thing at all. It shows that 'capital' is reaping all the rewards while 'labour' is getting the short end of the stick. And, of course, the growing income disparity only adds wind to the Marxists' sails.

Worryingly, this line of thinking could end up influencing politicians into doing something about the growing income disparity. If for no other reason than politicians have a massive vested interest in preventing some of the transformations currently being unleashed on our societies.

Indeed, as industrial jobs in the 'creative world' disappear (only to reappear in Mexico, China etc...), the job market in developed economies moves to a minority of very creative individuals who work for themselves, and a majority of fellows who work in the service industry for the creative minds and/or the tourists coming in from the industrial world.

This, of course, is a left wing politicians' worst nightmare, if for no other reason that their political parties (whether the Democratic Party, the Labour Party, the Spanish PSOE, the French PS...) all rely heavily on trade unions and organized labour for their funding, and to bring out the votes on election day. Should we be surprised that the most stringent attacks on globalization and free trade have moved from the far right to the soft left (remember when the US Democratic Party was a free trade party)?

As our countries de-industrialize, left-wing parties lose their bedrock of supports. Take the recent collapse of the AFL-CIO unions in the United States. Who would have thought such an event possible twenty years ago? And who could pretend that this will not have a big impact on the Democratic Party and its ability to win marginal constituencies in Ohio, Pennsylvania or Michigan? With the collapse of the unions, the Democratic Party loses what is most likely its most important pillar.

Nor is this trend likely to reverse itself, unless of course one turns to protectionism (a fact which might help explain Senator Schumer's rabid anti-China posturing). And beyond the left-wing parties, the new global re-organization of labour threatens the very existence of our welfare states.

Indeed, as the more creative people increasingly start to work for themselves, they look to base themselves in low tax environments. To some extent, this has already happened in the financial industry with the creation, every week, of dozens of new hedge funds. As a result, on any given day, the biggest foreign net buyer or seller of US Treasuries is the Caribbean Islands. Now needless to say, the Caribbean islanders are not amongst the world's largest investors; but the hedge funds domiciled there most definitely are. The 'efficiency capital' of the world which used to be domiciled in big investment banks, in the world's financial centres (whether London, New York, Frankfurt, Tokyo…) has now re-domiciled itself in hedge funds whose legal structures are in the Caymans, Bermuda, the British Virgin Islands. The tax revenue on the 'efficiency capital' is now lost for the US, the UK and others…and there is little those countries can do to gain it back.

As an increasing number of companies move to the 'platform-company' model (see *Our Brave New World*), it is likely that the top talent will want to work, or at least be taxed, in low tax environments. This will lead to a collapse in tax receipts in countries which do not adjust to this new model. In the new world towards which we are rapidly moving, income taxes will becoming increasingly voluntary and governments will have to get their pound of flesh through property and consumption taxes instead. This should lead to more efficient (i.e., downsized) governments all over the Western World. And we have a hard time believing that politicians of any party will welcome a downsizing in the government's importance. Globalization should end up killing off the Welfare State.

In the 'first wave' world of the agricultural revolution, governments basically provided subjects, who had little say in the matter anyway, a modicum of regalian functions (police, army, judges). With the second wave of the industrial revolution, governments started to branch out from their regalian functions and provided citizens with income redistribution, education, pensions, healthcare, unemployment insurance etc...But in the 'third wave' world of the knowledge economy, will governments still be able to provide 'prosumers' with all of the above services? How will they pay for them? In the 'third wave' world in which platform companies operate, taxes will increasingly become voluntary, hereby implying that governments will have to compete with each other to provide the best services at the lowest possible costs to attract the world's best platform companies, and their workers. Over time, this should mean that governments which provide the most efficient Regalian functions, and at the lowest possible costs (Hong Kong? Singapore? ...) stand to survive in their current structures. Others will have serious and challenging adjustments to make.

These facts lead us to question whether policymakers will take this "lying down"? Will governments try to redress the balance through taxation (i.e.: France's wealth tax), through regulations (i.e.: environmental constraints? Thirty-five hour work-week?...) or even outright protectionism?

Needless to say, the main consequence of such measures would be that both the rich and the poor would get poorer…a bad deal for the rich but a truly calamitous proposition for the poor.

But the fact that it is stupid doesn't mean that it can't happen (we learned as much from years of investing in Japan). Both protectionism and tax increases on the rich are very serious threats to the stability of our current system. And we should not discard these threats lightly. As income disparities continue to grow, and as politicians' power continues to erode, we may very well witness a political backlash in some countries.

Of course, we might be too alarmist here. Governments may not to do the wrong thing and could even end up doing the right thing. For example, governments could try to redress the income disparity imbalances by promoting share-ownership schemes through the entire structure of society (i.e.: Australia's super-annuation scheme, or Singapore's MPF plans…). This would ensure that even the workers toiling away at the lowest ranks of the economic ladder benefit from the "we take the profits, they take the jobs" trade.

Or, better yet, we can hope that the governments will step aside and continue to rely on the good services of Adam Smith's invisible hand in rectifying the growing wealth disparities.

# The "Invisible Hand" at Work

The ever-optimists in us want to believe that, for any given problem, the market, when left alone, will typically find a solution. The good news is that the birth of the platform company model, and the trend whereby Western companies say "we take the profits, you can have the jobs" has been so recent, and yet so powerful at the same time, that most governments have not had a chance to react to it (yet?). Thus, the market has been left free to do what it does best: adjust to new realities.

Assuming that we are right in our statement above that "the rich keep on getting richer" (and a lot of anecdotal evidence does point that way). Then it follows that whatever the rich buy should be going up in price much more rapidly than what poorer people buy (for there will be more competition for the goods/services that rich people buy). Incidentally, this has been one of the longest running themes of our research effort (Charles first started grumbling in 1999 that "it has never been so expensive to be rich"!).

As Anatole wrote in *The Times* back in the summer of 2005: "At its simplest, therefore, the disagreement over "true" inflation simply reflects people's tendency to focus on prices that are rising and forget about the ones that are going down. But the extent and persistence of the divergence between service and goods prices in the past decade also suggests a less obvious and more important story in three parts.

The first part of this story relates to China's entry into the global economy. By becoming the workshop of the world, China has pushed down the prices of all mass-produced manufactured goods. The virtually limitless supply of cheap labor and capital in China, and the chronic misallocations of capital will ensure that manufactured goods continue to get cheaper, not only in Britain but around the world.

But the relentless downward pressure on manufactured prices from China has resulted in a second effect which is less widely understood, even among economists: cheap imports from China have actually pushed up the prices of many goods and services which the Chinese cannot or do not produce-either because they lack the resources (for example, oil) or the legal infrastructure (financial services) or simply because some things cannot be traded (for example, housing, healthcare and education).

People who see China purely as a source of downward pressure on prices forget that overall inflation in any economy is essentially determined by the availability of money. If monetary policy is successfully run to produce an overall inflation rate of 2%, while the prices of manufactured goods are persistently falling by 3 or 4%, prices elsewhere in the economy must rise faster to maintain the 2% average inflation rate. In this sense the ever-cheaper consumer goods from China have created more leeway for other prices in the world economy to go up. This effect has been particularly visible in the prices of goods and services which the Chinese are ravenously consuming but cannot produce themselves-for example oil, financial services and luxury property around the world.

Which brings us to the third, and most surprising, part of the inflation story. As the prices of financial services and luxury goods are driven persistently higher, service-producing countries such as Britain or the US get richer relative to countries which specialize in manufacturing. And within Britain, the rich, who tend to work in high-end service industries which are relatively unaffected by competition from Asia, get richer, while the poor, who tend to work in industries more exposed to cheap-labor competition, get relatively poorer. For the lucky bankers, lawyers and, yes, even economic analysts, who are benefiting from this seismic change in the structure of the global economy, there is, however, a sting in the tail. While we are getting richer, the high-end services, most obviously housing, travel and private education-on which many of us spend a disproportionate share of our incomes are becoming more expensive, because of the very same global trends which are making us relatively rich.

That is why, even as inflation remains almost nonexistent, the talk in London's bars and restaurants is of galloping prices. Being rich has never been so expensive; and staying rich is going to get more exorbitant by the day.

Reading the above, our friend David Scott wrote a great report in which he stated that "while it has never been so expensive to be rich", it has also "never been so cheap to be poor". And, as ever with Scottie's report, there is a lot of truth behind that quip. Indeed, if we accept the crude simplification that poor people tend to spend more of their revenues on goods (which keep falling in price) while rich people spend more of their income on services (which seem to just keep on rising), then there might be a simple explanation to the impressive discontinuous inflation

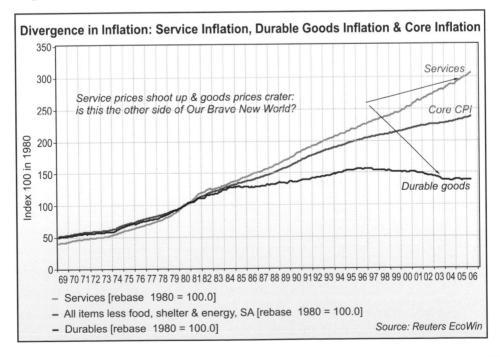

we have witnessed in recent years and which has baffled us such; the invisible hand is simply doing its work.

If the rich people in Western countries are currently capturing an inordinate amount of the World's profits, then those profits are slowly being taken back from them, either through higher service price inflation or through higher asset prices, especially prestige assets.

Take wine, art and horses as examples. As most of our readers will know, modern art, fine wines, & horses are assets that tend to peak just before the start of a pronounced downturn in the economic cycle. But lately, wine, art and horses seem to just keep on peaking! Prices have really been shooting up, breaking several records on the way:

- **The US$16 million horse.** In mid 2006, a two-year-old colt who had yet to run a race drew a world record sale price of US$16 million at an auction in Florida, after a furious bidding war between Englishman Michael Tabor and Sheikh Mohammed bin Rashid al Maktoum of Dubai (could he be thinking that horses will run better than Dubai stocks?). The sale broke the previous record of US$13.1 million paid in the mid-1980s for Seattle Dancer. Considering that very few horses ever reach winnings of US$1 million and that the all-time leading earner, Cigar, took home close to US$ 10 million, this is a truly mind-boggling price to pay for a horse that has yet to race a single race (incidentally, Seattle Dancer, the previous record holder, went on to win a paltry US$150,000, racing only five times in his short career).

- **The unbottled 2005 Bordeaux.** In the world of wine investments, Bordeaux is king, with up to US$3.7 billion worth of wines changing hands every year. Over the past twelve months, much to Charles' chagrin (Charles frequently says that he is now too old to drink cheap wines), the price of top vintages have surged more than +45%. Much of this latest rally can be attributed to the-yet to be bottled-2005 vintage. The 2005 vintage from some of the top chateaux are reportedly selling for around US$9,000 per case; as a comparison, in 2003, the same wines went for about US$3,800 per case... While investing in wine can be a very risky business, there is one undeniable advantage: if all else fails, it is a liquid asset...

- **The US$135 million portrait.** Also in mid 2006, Robert Lauder bought a portrait by Gustav Klimt for a staggering US$135 million, the highest sum ever paid for a painting, eclipsing a Picasso sold for US$104 million in 2004.

This odd dichotomy in inflation poses a hell of a quandary for policymakers. For a start, how does one measure inflation efficiently when all prices are either rising by +20% a year or falling by -15% a year? Churchill once said that economists use statistics like drunks use lampposts: for support more than for light. And given that there are so many statistics on inflation one might be able to back-up nearly any kind of preconceived idea with scientific sounding data.

Nevertheless, the simple fact remains that trying to get a clear picture for inflation today is a thankless task. But there is one thing we are convinced of: in our Western countries, the inflation rate for upper-class, and upper middle class people is very different than the inflation rate for lower class people.

And, needless to say, policymakers have to implement policies that ensure inflation remains low for poor people, not for rich people. Why? Well for a start, there are more poor people than rich people (which, incidentally, is why Mark Twain thought governments should tax the poor and not the rich). For seconds, poor people simply cannot afford inflation. Rich people can.

This brings us to a very important point, namely that if "it's different this time" for economic growth, then inflation isn't what it used to be! And comparing inflation rates across borders might not make much sense either.

Let us take China and the US as examples. In China, food costs still account for around 30% of the median family's monthly spending. This means that, when inflation hits 5% in China, it becomes a real problem very rapidly. After all, it's not like the median Chinese family can turn around and say: "Oh well; if a serving of rice now costs 10 RMB, then I'd rather not eat this week".

Meanwhile in the US, where the food bill has shrunk from 16% of income to 7% of income, when inflation accelerates, the consumer actually has more choice: he/she can decide not to go to the movies, take the bus instead of drive a car, postpone the purchase of the flat screen TV…

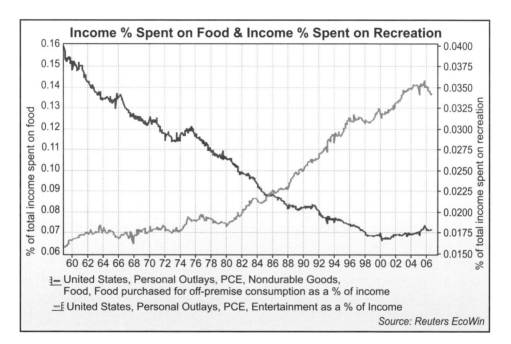

As an increasing percentage of our spending has become more discretionary, could inflation, as a direct consequence have become more subdued? When prices of non-essential items start to rise too much, the consumer in the western world has the option of pulling back thereby forcing prices lower down the road.

The difference in the spending composition of China and the US helps explain the very different policy approaches prevalent in both countries. In China, the government simply cannot afford to take the risk of

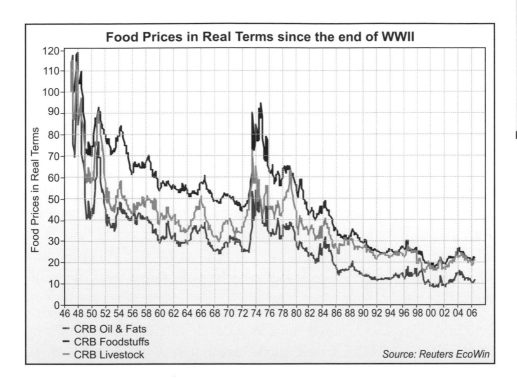

inflation; inflation would prove too devastating for the median family's lifestyle and could trigger riots and revolts. But in the US, policymakers can afford to be more relaxed for a pick up in food prices won't lead anyone to go hungry at the end of the month.

This simple fact brings us to the one reason we can think of which would see China, and other Asian nations, abandoning their mercantilist exchange rate policies: a sustained inflation problem. Indeed, as things stand, Asian nations have no real reason to modify their exchange rate policy; why shake up the status-quo since it works? However, if inflation was to appear in their economies, policy makers would have to rethink an exchange rate regime which forces them to print vast amount of money when they may not wish to do so. Moreover, and as we all appreciate, a rising currency is fundamentally a strong deflationary force (if for no other reason that everything one imports costs less).

Having said that, there is today in Asia no inflation problem to speak of. So the manipulation of exchange rates, with all of its consequences is likely to last for a while still.

At the risk of sounding Panglossian, we will admit that we are in awe at how Adam Smith's "invisible hand" works in strange and funny ways. If anyone had told us a decade ago that a "trade" would be put in place whereby China would say "give us all the jobs" and American companies would say "we'll take all the profits" and that this trade would lead to greater wealth, and greater social harmony in both countries, we most likely would have been very skeptical. Of course, we would have been wrong, for we would have forgotten to put our faith in Adam Smith's invisible hand which somehow has a way to make things work out in the end.

One interesting factor about the above developments is that they have occurred so quickly that politicians have not really had a chance yet to interfere with the invisible hand and turn gold into lead. However, listening to the rhetoric currently prevalent in the US Congress, some US politicians (Graham, Schumer...) seem very keen to catch up.

For this reason, and as explained in the previous chapter, we strongly believe that, at least as far as the US is concerned, the main risk of an implosion, or of the US causing the current "unstable world" to lose its balance, is of a political nature.

But can the same be said of Europe?

# Europe, a Possible "Breaking Point"?

In the chapters above we tried to show that:

- Asian central banks were manipulating their currencies.

- This manipulation created a subsidy to US consumption.

- It also encouraged companies to delocalize their production, a trend which, in turn, creates growing income disparities.

- With income disparity, inflation gets "out of whack".

- Without a serious pick-up in inflation in Asia, it is hard to see why Asian policymakers will change their FX policies.

- And, in turn, barring a major political mistake such as protectionism or tax increases, it is hard to see why the US consumer boom will implode.

- Interestingly, while in the US the "consumption subsidy" had been captured by an eager consumer, in Europe, the subsidy had been captured by spendthrift governments.

This brings us to our next point: while everyone wonders how sustainable the US consumer spending boom really is (and we tried to show that it was), few stop to question whether the European governments will be able to continue spending money like a drunk sailor on shore-leave in Bangkok.

Yet we believe that, today, this is one of the more important questions to ask.

For a start, consumer spending and government spending are two very different animals. Indeed, when the consumer can't get his hands on money, he typically tightens his belt and we have a recession. It is not much fun for anybody; but it is not the end of the world either. It is part and parcel of the economic cycle. A government, however, does not really have that option. When the economic cycle rolls over, the government does not have the option of "tightening its belt", especially not European governments whose welfare states include unemployment benefits, social security payments, subsidized housing, etc...

So what will happen if/when Asian policymakers decide to stop dishing out a subsidy to US consumption/European government spending? It seems to us that US consumers will have to tighten their belts (not the end of the world) and European governments will have to turn around and either: a) tighten their belts in the middle of an economic downturn (this, we believe, is practically impossible to do for any government, let alone the government of countries whose populations are happy to take to the street at the first hint of a supply-side reform); or b) get their pound of flesh from someone else. To some extent, this may already be happening.

Make no mistake about it: the "weak link" in our systems is not the US consumer. It is the European governments. And, should our reader doubt the assertion made above that Asian surpluses are financing European government spending, take a look at the following charts.

In recent years, we have seen very strong narrow money supply growth in Europe while money growth in the US and in Japan has been rather tame. This, of course, is somewhat surprising and goes against the common perceptions of a tight ECB, a trigger-happy Fed, and a clueless BoJ. So how do we explain it?

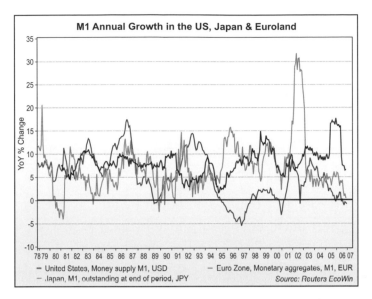

Simple really: the growth in M1 across Europe has to be compared to the rise of the weight of governments in the economy. Take France as an example (a country close to our hearts): over the past fifteen years, the weight of the government in the economy has increased; and the government has bought itself a spot at the table mostly through ever increasing budget deficits. So much so that government debt as a % of GDP has been climbing steadily, and accelerating as of late.

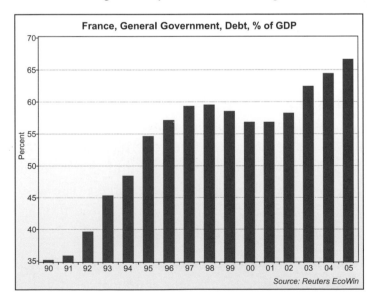

Needless to say, this debt needs to be financed, which means more government bonds; and these bonds can be bought by two kinds of investors:

- French/European institutions and French/European private savers.

- Foreign investors (Japanese institutions, Asian central banks, US or UK pension funds…).

If it is the first case, (the bonds are bought by French investors), then all the French government does is subsidize its state sectors, social security, etc... by picking the pockets of other French people. Overall, there is little impact on the French money supply (though obviously there is a big impact on growth since you are taking money from the productive private sector to put it in the unproductive public sector).

If it is the second case (the bonds are bought by foreigners), then M1 goes through the roof. In this instance, the French government drains money away from abroad (Japan? Hong Kong?...) and spends the money at home. Thus the rise in Europe's domestic monetary aggregates, in the face of ECB tightening, could simply be a sign that Europe's budget deficits are accelerating because of weak economic growth and that these budget deficits are increasingly financed from abroad.

As the purchasing of France's (or Italy's, or Portugal's, or Germany's…) government bonds by foreign institutions happens, France's money supply increases while the foreign institutions' countries' money supply shrinks (note the sharp drop in the Japanese monetary base in the past year). Money is being transferred from one place to the other. Against this decrease in money supply, however, we find an increase in assets: in our example, assets issued by France's government. This asset however, is nothing but a promise by France to pay, in the future, in French goods.

But then what happens when the new debt issued by France does not finance investments, able to increase the supply of goods for repayments in the future, but, instead, finances public consumption? Then more and more IOUs are issued while the productive capacity to honor these IOUs does not increase.

When a country is in this situation, more often than not, the adjustment is taken by the currency. As Jacques Rueff famously said: *The currency (exchange rate) is the sewer that collects all unearned rights.* But that, of course, is assuming that the currency can take the adjustment!

Let us take Argentina as a recent example of how things can go pear-shaped rapidly. Argentina had a fixed exchange rate with the US Dollar, operating within the constraint of a currency board. At the same time, local provinces and the central government could borrow freely in the international markets.

Now a currency board works if the local money supply moves according to the variations in the foreign exchange reserves, themselves a function of the current account surpluses or deficits (i.e.: Hong Kong). But if reserves, and money supply, are allowed to rise as the country moves increasingly into debt, then all bets are off! For a while, we have a boom in public consumption, but at some point the market gets wary…and then it all ends in tears.

If anything in our global system today is "unsustainable", (and we are not sure that there is), we would tend to believe that it is the European government borrowing.

In Euroland today, a number of countries exhibit high, and rising *primary* deficits (Italy, Greece, Portugal…). These deficits are partly financed by selling debt to foreign institutions (Japanese banks, US pension funds, Chinese Central Bank). And given that, following the collapse of the Growth & Stability Pact, there are now no more rules to cap the growth of budget deficits, there is a risk that the ECB will be unable to regain control of money supply growth. Money supply growth in Europe could explode, but would mostly rise for the benefit of public entities (government spending, money-losing public services etc…).

In such a turn of events, what could the ECB do?

The ECB could raise short rates, though that would certainly not be the solution. Higher rates would push into bankruptcy all negative cash-flow activities in Euroland (including real estate, one of the few bright spots), and thus lead to bigger budget deficits, and more unemployment. Moreover it would attract more of the international, yield-chasing "hot money", leading to a further rise in money supply and a rise in the exchange rate (which would depress the economy even more).

The ECB's hands are now tied: without some kind of a self-imposed control on budget policies of underlying nations, there is no hope that the Euroland monetary policy can be controlled by the ECB. In other words, this means that the future of the European experience, and the survival of the Euro as a viable currency are now in the hands of Prodi, Zapatero, Chirac and Merkel.

And if that was not enough of a disturbing thought, consider where we go from here.

In recent years, foreigners have been buying European bonds, and the Euro, massively. Partly because it was going up, partly because it offered higher interest rates than the US$ (though no longer), partly because some US$ earners (Venezuela, Iran, Russia...) wanted to own anything but US$, and partly because investors panicked about the US trade deficits. This buying led to a rising exchange rate, a collapse in quality premiums, and an expanding money supply across Europe.

But what if these trends start reversing? If foreigners decide to sell the Euro, European money supply growth will implode, and, with it economic activity and the ability of European governments to raise further financing. Indeed, as the Euro starts to fall, it is likely that investors will all of a sudden realize that governments only go bust when they issue debt in a currency that they can't print. In the past ten years, France government debt to GDP has moved from 35% in French Franc (i.e.: a currency the government could print at will) to 67% in Euros (i.e.: a currency that only the ECB can print).

# Europe's Obvious Weak Link: Italy

Of course, at this stage, rather than throw around blanket accusations against European "poli-tics" (poli because there are too many and tics because they are as fun as blood sucking insects), it makes sense to qualify what we mean when we refer to as "European governments". After all, placing in the same bag the governments of Spain or Holland, and those of France, Germany or Italy doesn't make much sense. If nothing else, one fundamental factor that explains the divergent performance of Italy and Spain is the different nature of their respective governments.

Spain, partly because of the national consensus in favour of rapid economic development after the Franco era, has developed a pragmatic and broadly pro-market approach to government. Deregulation of banks and financial institutions in the early 1990s set off booms in construction and consumer borrowing, which have kept the economy rapidly growing and allowed labour markets to be gradually deregulated without too much controversy or pain.

In Italy, by contrast, the government has evolved into a totally predatory force. The raison d'être of government, as most Italians see it, is to plunder resources from the private sector in order to support public employees and maintain the privileges of politically powerful groups. Italian politicians blatantly abuse idealistic claims about "social solidarity" and support of the poor to subsidise privileged lobbies, such as civil servants or unionized workers.

Needless to say, there is nothing unusual about governments and politicians behaving in a self-serving manner, but what is unique in Italy is the transparency with which politicians prey on their citizens without offering them anything of value in return. Like Romulus and Remus, Italy's politicians seem to be descended from she-wolves–and Italian citizens and businesses feel entitled to treat their government in return as a totally predatory force. Not only do they go to extraordinary lengths to avoid paying taxes, but they mirror the lupine nature of government in the way they deal with officialdom themselves. Just as the politicians loot private citizens for the benefit of their own political interests, so do Italian citizens shamelessly plunder and exploit the political system whenever they get the chance.

This mutual exploitation between the government and its citizens is always in evidence in Italy, whether in the self-serving media legislation of Silvio Berlusconi, or the political abuse of the office of President of the European Commission by Romano Prodi, or the dubious dealings between the former Governor of the Bank of Italy and the country's commercial banks. Such is the mutual hostility between the citizens and the government that Italy can fairly be described as the world's only prosperous "failed state".

However, unlike Somalia, Afghanistan or Haiti, Italy is a country with a long intellectual history, a rich culture, and deep commercial traditions. It created an advanced economy without requiring the services of an effective Nation State. As long as the politicians stayed in the background, the private sector was able to power the economy, and until the 1990s, Italy's entrepreneurial economy went from strength to strength. Italians households became the world's richest savers and the leading clients for private banks across Europe. Italy was also, until recently, Europe's biggest market for retail investment funds. Meanwhile, the Italian government simply printed money to subsidise its supporters and periodically stole some resources from the private sector through devaluation and inflation.

But at some point in the future, the viability of this arrangement may be put into question. Italy's tragedy is that membership of the Euro has destroyed the predatory but sustainable arrangement mentioned above. The Euro forces Italian politicians to loot their economy more aggressively than ever, since they can no longer print money to subsidise their supporters. In 2007, this process may reach its logical conclusion, as the government raises taxes and cuts services, while private enterprise sinks deeper into a recession. In turn, this will only increase the demand for even higher taxes in 2008. Whether Italy will be able to survive this process without breaking out of the Euro is a question which could increasingly be asked. At the very least, it should be a question that the large buyers of Italian debt in the Asian central banks and elsewhere should be pondering.

After all, what option will the Italian government have when the next slowdown or recession comes around?

In Japan, when the economy slowed after the 1990 bust, the government stepped in and spending went through the roof. The government issued a lot of JGBs to finance its spending. And, conveniently, if the market looked like it might not want extra JGBs, the BoJ was there to absorb them. Throughout the late 1990's, we saw the BoJ time and again intervening in the markets to ensure that yields remained low.

But will the Italian government be able to tell the ECB to buy its bonds? Remember that Italy has repeatedly been in breach of its treaty obligations (i.e.: no deficit higher than–3% of GDP) and that the ECB is most unlikely to look kindly on any request Italy might present.

In 2001, the Argentine government could not tell the US Fed to print more money in order to roll-over its debt and so Argentina went bust. Japan was always able to tell the BoJ to print Yen and buy JGBs, and so ten year Japanese yields fell to 0.42% in 2003.

Today, the whole of the Sovereign debt of Italy has been issued in a currency which is not under the control of the Italian Ministry of Finance.

Nor is there a European Ministry of Finance. So, in a hypothetical crisis, either the ECB decides to play nice, and buy everybody's government bonds, in which case interest rates fall (and the Euro tanks). Or the ECB decides to stick to its mandate, in which case real interest rates rise, the Euro shoots up and activity in Europe implodes.

So which way will the ECB lean? The question is not academic. Today, Italy has a debt to GDP equivalent to 105% of its GDP. If interest rates on that debt are at 4% (as they are today) and the nominal GDP grows at 2% (as it does today in a period of global synchronized boom) then an increasing part of the Italian GDP is being captured simply to service the debt. Moreover, if nominal rates compound in Italy at 4% and nominal GDP compounds at 2%, then one does not need a Nobel Prize in economics to deduct that, at some point, bankruptcy is unavoidable; the "awesome power" of compounding interest rates must lead to an Italian bankruptcy.

On the intra-European comparisons if, in Spain, interest rates are at 4%, but nominal growth is at 5.5%, the debt burden of Spain will keep falling, (while it will keep rising in Italy). This should lead to a massive opening in spreads between the good signatures (Spain, Holland, etc…) and the bad signatures (Italy, Portugal, etc…). This means that the cost of capital will go up in Italy, and down in Spain. All things being equal, capital spending should then collapse in Italy and go through the roof in Spain. Unemployment should explode in Italy and contract massively in Spain, etc…

Of course, massive divergences in costs of capital and availability of labor have occurred within countries throughout History (i.e.: differences between South East and North East England) and have not always led to implosion. In fact, differences in growth typically lead to population migrations (i.e.: if people can't find jobs in Michigan, they move to California).

But will the Italians move en masse to Spain? Will the Germans move to Holland? Given that most European countries' population are getting older, that seems unlikely. Indeed, immigration is a thing that young people do (though we do love the story of the 93 year old Jewish grandmother immigrating to the US from Germany in 1934 who, when asked by the customs official why she was immigrating at such an advanced age replied: "there is no future for me in Germany"). Older folks tend to get set in their ways and do not move around (more on that later).

The other option for Europe to harmonize the differences in economic growth is to tax the wealth creating regions, and re-distribute the money to the wealth destroying regions (i.e.: in the US, the Federal government might take money out of Texas and plow it back into West Virginia). But under the current European political structure, taxing Spain's growth to pay for Italy's bust is simply not an option; which Spanish politicians will want to stand for office on the slogan "let's tax Barcelona to send money to Napoli"? (Admittedly, the slogan might work better in Italy).

So what will happen for Italy? Will the ECB cave in and bring in low rates? Will Italy experience a bankruptcy? Or will Italy exit from the Euro?

# CHAPTER 17

# Could Italy Leave the Euro?

*Divorce, Italian Style* was a 1962 movie in which Marcello Mastroianni plays a Sicilian nobleman married to an ugly, bullying and financially ruinous harridan, from whom he desperately wants to disengage. Unfortunately, he has no legal way to do this, since the Italian legal system made no provisions for divorce. His only recourse is therefore to kill his wife.

This movie is, of course, a perfect allegory for the Italian and European economies forty years later. Italy today is under the thumb of an ugly, oppressive and financially ruinous harridan called the Euro. The concept of divorce, separation or withdrawal does not exist under EU law. What, then, is Italy to do?

The fiscal arithmetic which makes Italy's position in a deflationary euro-zone economically questionable is highlighted above. Moreover, politically, the charge that the euro is responsible for Italy's economic problems is superficially quite easy to sustain (even if it is not actually true). Until 1997, when the socialist government (led by Prodi) took Italy into the euro, Italy was the fastest growing major economy in Europe, consistently outperforming both Germany and France. Since 1998 it has lagged in every single year behind France and in all but two years behind Germany.

Starting with these economic and political premises one can arrive at a conclusion that the country's continuing membership of the euro-zone could become politically incompatible with the present monetary conditions.

Interestingly, if Italy left the euro, the government's long-term bonds would continue to pay the present interest rate of just 3.5%, but now in lira instead of euros. Italy's liabilities would be converted from a strong currency over which it has no control, into a weak currency which it can print at will without any cost to the government or compensating payment to its creditors. This may seem unfair and even fraudulent, but such are the prerogatives of sovereign governments–legal opinion and historical precedent are both quite clear on this point (see below).

To maximize the benefit from this effective debt default, the Italian government would, of course, need to lock in today's euro interest rates for as long as possible by extending the maturity of its debts before exiting the euro. Interestingly, this is exactly what the Italian government has been doing. Italy's average debt maturity is now over 5 years, roughly twice as long as in 1999. A sensible exit strategy for Italy would be to extend this maturity to 10 years or beyond. Luckily for Italy, investors are willing to buy unlimited quantities of long bonds denominated in euros at 3.5% yields.

Now imagine that the Italian government managed to fix all of its debts for 10 years at 3.5%. It would then face an almost irresistible temptation to ditch the euro. For suppose that long-term rates on the "New Lira" shot up to 10% immediately after devaluation. The market value of the government's 3.5% debt would instantly be reduced to just 59 cents on the dollar. The market value of Italy's government debt would fall instantly to a manageable 70% of GDP and Italy's fiscal problems would be solved at a stroke.

Looking further ahead, Italians might have to pay higher interest rates on future borrowings. But given that Italy has the world's highest savings rate and very little debt in the private sector, this should not matter too much. The country's fiscal problems are really due to the accumulation of past obligations and breaking out of the euro could ease this burden overnight.

In sum, the potential benefits of exiting the euro are quite substantial–and the direct costs may well be smaller than generally believed. But does this mean that a rational government would decide to take the plunge, delaying only for as long as is needed to stretch out the duration of the national debt? Not necessarily, because a third option exists which is clearly preferable to both the exit strategy and continuation of the status quo. This is to stay in the euro, but to persuade (or blackmail) the other members and the European Central Bank to pursue aggressive pro-growth policies across the euro zone as a whole.

Indeed, we are fairly convinced that, come the next economic downturn, one of two things will happen. Either the European Central Bank will have to ease monetary policy decisively to make economic conditions easier for Italy to live with–or Italy will withdraw from the euro zone.

Now the ECB's official statements on monetary policy-that a cut in interest rates or a devaluation would have no effect on economic conditions–are just content-free propaganda: Soviet-style ideology designed to justify whatever happens to be the current policy of the ECB. This is clear not only from common sense but also from the econometric simulations based on past behaviour. As the ECB proves slow to ease in a downturn (a fairly safe bet), Italians will be tempted to start rattling their chains and seriously threaten disengagement–which brings us to the question of why an Italian withdrawal should be taken seriously, even though monetary divorce in Europe is not allowed.

To understand this issue we must focus on two unprecedented features of today's monetary arrangements. The first is that the Italian government has, in theory, given up forever a fundamental right of any sovereign country–the right to determine what will constitute legal tender within its own borders. The second is that international investors have assumed this decision to be genuinely irreversible simply because the Maastricht Treaty says it is.

The strange financial result of these two aberrations is that the spread between Italian and German government bond yields is only 20 basis points and that many European banks–unprofitable German mortgage banks in particular–have invested hundreds of billions of euros on a leveraged basis to pick up the very modest, but apparently risk-free, profits from buying Italian bonds and going short of their German equivalents.

As a consequence, a decision by the Italian government to withdraw from the euro-or even a perception by investors that such a decision might conceivably be threatened by the Italian government sometime in the not too distant future-would trigger a financial crisis of monstrous proportions not only (or even mainly) in Italy, but throughout the euro zone.

But could Italy credibly threaten to recreate its own currency? So powerful is the dogma that withdrawal is impossible that only two legal scholars have ever seriously examined this issue. They are Professor Hal S. Scott of Harvard Law School (whose 1998 article "*When the Euro Falls Apart*" can be found on the web in the December 1998 issue of *International Finance*) and Dr Charles Proctor of the London law-firm Nabarro Nathanson, editor of *Mann on the Legal Aspect of Money*, a book described by central bankers as "the Bible" of international monetary law. The latest edition of this book, published by Oxford University Press, contains a new chapter on withdrawal from the Eurozone, which offers the most detailed and thorough analysis of how withdrawal could happen and what it might mean for financial contracts of various kinds.

These two authorities differ substantially in their approach and anyone interested in this subject in detail (which ought to mean anyone with a substantial position in the euro, European bank shares or Italian bonds) should read both the articles mentioned above for themselves. Cutting through the detail, there are three points of clear legal consensus which are of huge significance to financial markets:

## 1- Withdrawal Is Possible

Despite the prohibitions against re-creating national currencies in the EU Treaties, the Italian government *would* have the legal ability to reissue its own currency, even though this would obviously entail financial and economic risks. Sovereign governments can withdraw from treaties, even when some of the provisions purport to be "irrevocable", as in the case of the monetary union. The normal way to do this is to amend the treaty, but for this to happen all the other signatories (in this case all the other euro members) would have to agree to allow Italy to withdraw. Such a negotiated withdrawal would sweep away most of the legal obstacles. But what if the other members refused to let Italy leave?

Politically such refusal is hard to imagine. Would other European countries really try to stand in the way of a democratic decision made by the Italian government, especially if this were backed by a referendum? Would Europe's governments deny the Italians a right which Gorbachev granted to the citizens of the former Soviet Union? This seems unlikely.

Nevertheless another option for withdrawal exists. Italy could simply declare unilaterally that it would start printing a New Lira. This action would obviously be in breach of the Maastricht Treaty and would be open to challenge in the European Court of Justice, but it would almost certainly be upheld by Italian courts. The question is what would happen to Italy's domestic and international obligations?

## 2- Euro Obligations Redenominated into New Lira

In the event of a negotiated withdrawal, there is no doubt that the government would be entitled to rewrite Italian financial contracts, including its own bond obligation, into New Lira. Investors who claimed to be defrauded by such a "redenomination" could expect no support from British or American courts.

The principle of *lex monetae*, a well-established rule of international law which says that monetary contracts should be interpreted by all courts as if they were applying the laws of the issuing country, unless there is specific evidence that the contract was intended to be governed by some foreign law. This means that the judgment of Italian courts as regards domestic securities would be recognised and upheld by other jurisdictions. Because Italian government bonds are issued unequivocally under Italian domestic law, they would be regarded as contracts between Italian residents regardless of who happens to own these bonds today. So courts in London and New York would uphold Italy's right to redenominate government bonds, provided the Italian courts did not strike down the entire currency reform. On the other hand, bonds issued under overseas law-e.g.: Eurobonds under English law or securities under New York law, might not be redenominated and would continue to be paid in euros.

But what if Italy pulled out of the euro unilaterally? What if the government created the New Lira by passing a monetary law that was clearly in breach of the (unamended) EU Treaties and therefore illegal under European law? This scenario would create huge uncertainties for investors (and huge opportunities for lawyers). It is impossible to say exactly what would happen.

### 3- Default Swaps Offer No Protection Against Redenomination

Standard default swaps would offer no protection to investors in Italian bonds and other financial contracts, because a negotiated withdrawal and redenomination would not be interpreted by any court as "an event of default". Holders of default swaps might have a slightly stronger case in the event of a *unilateral* withdrawal, but they would still find it very difficult to get paid.

Detailed discussion of these arguments is probably still premature– and in any case should be left to lawyers–but the financial and policy implications are clear enough: If the possibility of an Italian withdrawal were ever taken seriously by the markets, foreign holders of Italy's €1.5 trillion public debt would face enormous losses. With nearly 50% of the Italian public debt held overseas, a good chunk of it by European banks on a leveraged basis with a zero capital-weighting, the potential losses from an Italian redenomination would be big enough to endanger the solvency of the entire euro-zone banking system. In other words, the

Italian government is now in a position to kill the Euro and wreck the European banking system merely by *threatening* to withdraw.

The most likely result of such a threat would be to force the ECB to ease policy and encourage a weaker Euro, in order to accommodate the Italian government's demands. This would certainly be a rational response from the ECB.

But what if the ECB failed to play ball? Or what if Italy's economic conditions, following the coming tax hikes, deteriorate further? The government could then become desperate enough to start openly demanding a monetary easing and devaluation, as it did in 1992. That time round, the Bundesbank decided to ignore the Italian (and British) entreaties and orchestrated the expulsion of the Lira and the Pound from the ERM. This time, however, the balance of power is tilted the other way. The Italian government can blackmail the ECB with the threat of withdrawal and a European banking crisis.

The ECB's top priorities would then be to prevent a collapse of the entire Euro project or a solvency crisis among the German/European banks. Given this shift in the balance of power it seems almost inevitable that the Italians would win the confrontation and that the ECB would have to ease.

Of course, at present, such speculations are still just fantasy, or at least economic science fiction. But anybody who still believes that a break-up of the Euro is impossible should at least re-examine this assumption with a skeptical eye. Experience shows that, in confrontations between politics and financial markets, events sometimes move from impossible to inevitable without ever passing through improbable.

Investors who want to be better prepared for the "impossible" than they were before the 1992 European currency crisis should contact Oxford University Press for a copy of *Mann and the Legal Aspect of Money* (those who can't face a 900-page legal textbook, should at least rent a video of *Divorce Italian Style*).

In any event, Italy's precarious position within a shoddily-built, politically motivated, Euro monetary experience is certainly a question mark as to the "sustainability" of the current global financial arrangements. And unfortunately, Italy is not the only dark horse in Europe.

# Will the Real France Please Stand Up?

This coming May will see the unfolding of the presidential election in France. Three candidates have a serious shot at being in the second round (Segolene Royal, Nicolas Sarkozy and Jean-Marie Le Pen) and only two (Royal and Sarkozy) have a hope of gaining the presidency.

This election, we believe, will turn out to be very important in that it will mark which France is the most important numerically: communist France, or capitalist France. Let us explain.

In France today, the observer can find two systems of production that co-exist in an uneasy cooperation: a capitalist system, and a communist one. Unfortunately, in recent years and under Mr Chirac, the communist system of production in France has been growing at a much faster pace than the capitalist one. And alarmingly, the incomprehension between the two systems (as highlighted by the strike against the "Contrat Premier Emploi" to get young people into jobs) is as wide in France today as it has ever been.

To quickly summarize the characteristics of a Marxist system, we will use a Marxist grid, looking at how the factors of production (Capital and Labour) are allocated, and then how the external world, the "user", is serviced.

## 1) Capital in the Marxist Grid

- There is no such thing as a cost of capital.
- Interest rates have no function in such an economy.

- Returns on capital are not considered before making an investment.
- Profits are never a part of the picture.
- Capital is available either through direct access to the government budget or through borrowing, usually through government guarantees.
- There are no bankruptcies.
- Savings have no return.

## 2) Labour in the Marxist Grid

- Labour is exploitation, and must be avoided.
- Labour is fungible (all workers are equal, i.e. not worth a lot, and can be replaced indiscriminately).
- Life employment is the rule; career movements are made according to age and/or personal involvement in the unions or the party.
- Unions are heavily subsidized by the government. The work force has no choice but to join the unions.
- There is no such thing as a productivity gain accruing to the users.

## 3) Relation Between the Production System and the Outside World

- Prices are not there to clear the market, but are fixed by government or administrative decrees.
- In theory, demand is regulated by administrative means, or by laws.
- In practice, excess demand emerges and we have queues. Otherwise, we have lack of demand, leading to overcapacity and waste.
- Competition is in principle not accepted. As a result, there is no such thing as a "client". A client can move to a different provider, which implies the existence of a competitive environment. A "user" cannot.

If we decide to apply the criteria outlined above to the French economy, we discover pretty quickly that quite a few sectors are operating, partly or totally, according to those rules. As we look at it, the French communists sectors are:

- The health system (hospitals, social security, pensions, etc…)
- The educational system
- The public transportation system
- General & Local Administrations
- Energy & Waste Management
- The postal system
- The telecom system

The next step is of course to try to evaluate the relative weight of these sectors in the French GDP. Our methodology will be very simple: the GDP is the sum of the value-added by all the participants in an economy. Through the French national accounts, we have access to the added values of each individual sectors, including the above "communist sectors".

If we subtract the value added by these "communist sectors" from the French GDP, we will have a rough idea of the split between the communist and non communist sectors. Of course, it will be imprecise, but, as Keynes said, we would rather be roughly correct than precisely wrong.

The first fact to emerge is that, since 1978, the French communist economy has grown far more than the capitalist one. On average, the communist sectors have grown by 2.8% per annum while the private sector has grown by 0.8% per annum. The second fact to emerge from this breakdown is that, since 1978 again, the communist sectors have never had one single recession! Meanwhile, the capitalist sectors have had to endure five recessions. No wonder everyone in France wants to be a civil servant: it pays more, the growth is higher and there are no risks of unemployment.

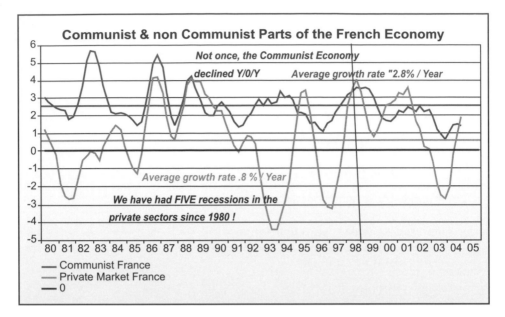

**Communist & non Communist Parts of the French Economy**

*Not once, the Communist Economy declined Y/O/Y*  *Average growth rate "2.8% / Year*

*Average growth rate .8 % / Year*

*We have had FIVE recessions in the private sectors since 1980 !*

'80 '81 '82 '83 '84 '85 '86 '87 '88 '89 '90 '91 '92 '93 '94 '95 '96 '97 '98 '99 '00 '01 '02 '03 '04 '05

— Communist France
— Private Market France
— 0

But is this state of affairs sustainable? Could we soon be getting to the point that Brezhnev described in 1980 when he said: "they pretend to work, and we pretend to pay them?".

Since 1945, France has been under an unspoken sharing of power: the Right and the Socialists would fight for political power. Meanwhile, control of the communist economy would be vested in the hands of the unions (CGT, CGT-FO or CFLT). These communists (CGT) and Trotskyites unions (CGT-FO) more or less control all the sectors we have identified above as the communist sectors. The impressive growth of the communist system we also reviewed above was only made possible by a constant transfer from the non communist to the communist economy through ever increasing subsidies (taxation) and debt. In turn, these transfers led to a structurally declining growth rate of the whole of the French economy, and to a solid accumulation of debt (French government debt is now a solid 67% of GDP).

However, one day, the French economy will start falling in absolute terms, simply because the private sector will no longer be able to finance the communist economy.

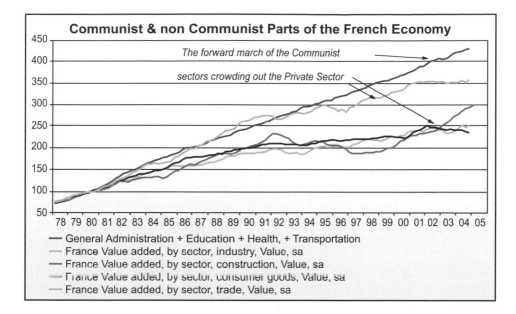

**Communist & non Communist Parts of the French Economy**

*The forward march of the Communist*

*sectors crowding out the Private Sector*

— General Administration + Education + Health, + Transportation
— France Value added, by sector, industry, Value, sa
— France Value added, by sector, construction, Value, sa
— France Value added, by sector, consumer goods, Value, sa
— France Value added, by sector, trade, Value, sa

And that day, France will confront a massive political crisis; the government willingly or unwillingly, will have to go for the clash, as Mrs. Thatcher did with the miners, or President Reagan did with the air-traffic controllers.

Last year, we experienced a few skirmishes when PM Villepin presented his very mild labour market reforms. Before he knew it, every other student was on the streets of France, blocking traffic and preventing people from going to work. We believe that these were the opening salvos of a "battle" which could end up being very long and very bloody for all participants.

Undeniably, the real fight has not even started. But we nevertheless know quite a few things:

1.  Present trends are unsustainable

2.  They will end with a major political clash

3.  While we are certain that the clash will happen, we are not convinced about our timing (very modestly, we will point out that Von-Mises and Hayek explained very convincingly that the Soviet Union

could not work and that it would therefore collapse in the 1920s & 1930s....)

4.  There is no certainty that the fight will be won by the "free economy" (i.e.: Argentina, Venezuela...)

5.  The trends that we have highlighted in this paper have not gone unnoticed in the French capitalist sectors. Our work with French companies re-enforces our belief that a number of small French companies have already delocalized and that a number of big companies are also considering a move

6.  If French companies are thinking of moving, then French "capitalists" are everyday packing their bags. In fact, the widespread quoted number is that at least one high net worth Frenchman leaves the country every day to settle in Britain, Switzerland, Belgium...As a result, and for the first time ever, more than one million French citizens are living abroad. The countries where Frenchmen have moved to in hordes (US, UK, Switzerland, Asia...) are indicative of what they are looking for. The new entrepreneurs are moving to the Anglo-Saxon world, to be able to create. The old entrepreneurs who have been successful, are moving to Switzerland or Belgium, to avoid the punitive French tax rates.

Investors investing in the "sustainability" of the European business model could, we fear, be disappointed.

# Beyond Poli-Tics, Europe's Demographic Challenge

In *A Study of History,* Toynbee contends that historical movements are the consequences of the challenges confronting a society, the role of the elite being to analyze the challenge and find appropriate responses. If the challenge is tackled successfully, the society progresses and finds a new equilibrium. If the answers are not the right ones, the challenge returns, until such a time as the elite can be replaced (revolution) or the society itself disappears (end of civilisation).

This analysis was very relevant to Europe between 1860 and 1960 when the challenge was nationalism and the Franco-German rivalry. After three wars did not settle the problem, a new elite (Monnet, Schuman, Adenauer) rose to the forefront and came up with European integration.

Today, Europe faces a very serious challenge of a completely different nature. Europe's challenge is certainly not the old Franco-German rivalry, with Britain arbitraging. The challenge is demographic and sociological in nature: how to make an old and rich society co-exist with young, poor and desperate societies, in the same geographic zones, in the knowledge that there can be no military solution? The implosion of social welfare systems, immigration, internal troubles, deteriorating educational systems...all of these problems are rooted to some extent in the demographic collapse of Western Europe.

Indeed, Europe today faces three concomitant demographic challenges:

- **The Ageing of the Baby Boom Generation**

- **The Lengthening of Life-Spans** (and the associated medical costs of keeping people in old age alive for longer)

- **A Sharp Drop in Fertility Rates** (in a number of European countries, women now have less than two children)

The combination of the above three factors imply that, on a relatively short-term horizon, most of Europe's welfare states will go bankrupt. And, unfortunately, polishing up the old solutions of further European integration (as is now happening in Brussels) that worked for the purpose of keeping Europe at peace does very little to solve this precise challenge. Focusing on the wrong question (e.g. France's obsession with "l'exception culturelle") is also of little help.

We do not know how the European elites will react but we do know that defensive answers (protectionism) will not succeed. Tackling a historical challenge requires imagination, optimism and courage; and on these qualities, we venture to say that the current batch of European leaders do not score high marks.

As we look at it, the only way for Europe's welfare-states to survive is for either:

- Europe to accept far greater migratory flows from Eastern Europe, Turkey, Asia, North Africa and Africa than it already does; or

- The baby-boomers to accept that the age of retirement will need to be pushed back

Is the acceptance of massive migratory flows likely in countries such as France who believe that work is there to be shared (i.e.: the 35 hour-week)? As of today, the signs look ominous.

We tend to believe that the only hope for Europe is on the retirement front; in other words, that the retirement age will be pushed back pretty much everywhere (incidentally, this has started to occur in Scandinavia).

Hopefully, as baby boomers retire, spouses everywhere will realize (as Charles' wife did when Charles retired from Alliance Capital) that having a retired husband is "less money and more husband–the worst of both worlds" and push them back out into the workforce.

Otherwise, Europe is in trouble. Can the European welfare states really survive the ageing of their underlying populations (especially if their more productive knowledge workers high-tail it to lower tax jurisdictions such as London, Geneva or Hong Kong)?

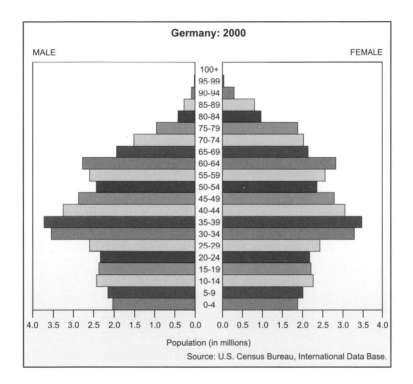

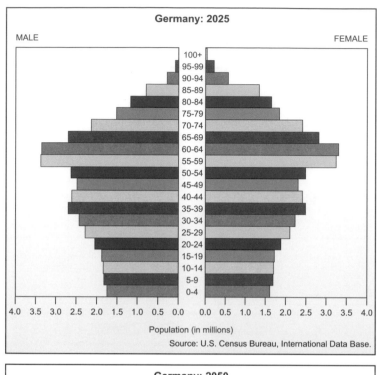

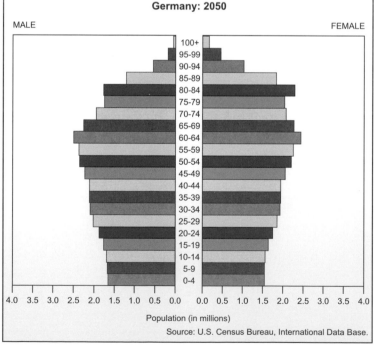

# CHAPTER 20

# Tails I Win a Little, Heads I Lose a Lot

In the previous chapter, we tried to establish the following points:

- Asian central banks were still very busy manipulating their exchange rates.

- Unless we started to see a serious pick-up in inflation, the Asian central banks would likely continue to manipulate their currencies.

- By manipulating their currencies, Asian central banks distort a number of prices around the World.

- The most obvious and visible distortion is the large subsidy to the US consumer.

- Most investors fear that this subsidy to the US consumer is unsustainable and will end in a big financial accident. We have tried to show that worrying about a meltdown in the US consumer was a waste of time.

- A less obvious distortion is the subsidy to European governments.

- If one is looking for "unsustainability" anywhere in the system, then this could be it. The European governments may not be able to continue to spend more than they earn, and increase their overall debt levels, while remaining bound within the rules of the Euro.

More often than not, investing successfully is not about picking winners, but about avoiding losers. And this is why we spend most of our time looking for investments that offer a "Tails: I win, and heads: I don't lose" proposition.

There is little doubt in our minds that identifying such asset classes today is a very challenging proposition. Indeed, should the financial system that we currently live in and describe above start to crack (whether because Asian central banks stop manipulating their currencies, or because the European political construction exercise crumbles under the weight of its own contradictions, or because (against our belief) the US consumer really does hit the wall with a "thump") then a number of asset classes would adjust very violently. And frankly, figuring out which way each asset class would adjust in the different scenarios is extremely challenging.

Nevertheless, with the decision tree below, we try to identify asset classes that would offer a "tails I win, heads I don't lose" proposition (in other words, if there is no shock to the system, I continue to make money... and if there is a shock the system, then I walk away without too much damage). We should also try to identify the asset classes that would be

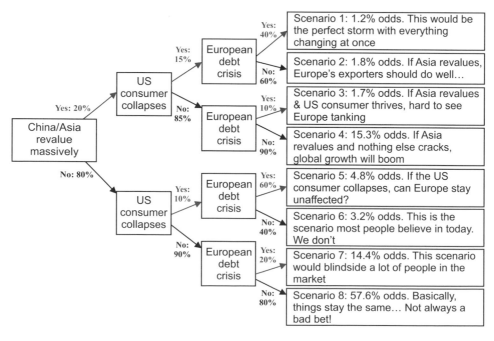

"heads I win, tails I lose big time" for those are the asset classes we probably want to avoid, or even short to hedge ourselves against a shock to the current system.

NB: In the decision tree above, we put what we believe are the odds of each event…but of course, our reader might wish to place different odds on each event

And what would these various scenarios mean for the various asset classes? (red is bad, grey is good)

| | Scenario 1 | Scenario 2 | Scenario 3 | Scenario 4 | Scenario 5 | Scenario 6 | Scenario 7 | Scenario 8 |
|---|---|---|---|---|---|---|---|---|
| | Asia revalues, US tanks, EMU tanks | Asia revalues, US tanks, EMU is fine | Asia revalues, US is fine, EMU tanks | Asia revalues, US is fine, EMU is fine | Asia fixes FX, US tanks, EMU tanks | Asia fixes FX, US tanks, EMU is fine | Asia fixes FX, US is fine, EMU tanks | Asia fixes FX, US is fine, EMU is fine |
| Odds | 1.2% | 1.8% | 1.7% | 15.3% | 4.8% | 3.2% | 14.4% | 57.6% |
| US Long Dated Bonds | | | | | | | | |
| EMU Long Dated Bonds | | | | | | | | |
| Japan Long Dated Bonds | | | | | | | | |
| Asia Long Dated Bonds | | | | | | | | |
| Quality Corporate Debt | | | | | | | | |
| Distressed Debt | | | | | | | | |
| Emerging Market Debt | | | | | | | | |
| US Equities | | | | | | | | |
| Euro Equities | | | | | | | | |
| Japan Equities | | | | | | | | |
| Asian Equities | | | | | | | | |
| Emerging Market Equities | | | | | | | | |
| US$ | | | | | | | | |
| EURO | | | | | | | | |
| JPY | | | | | | | | |
| GBP | | | | | | | | |
| CHF | | | | | | | | |
| CA$ | | | | | | | | |
| SEK | | | | | | | | |
| SG$ | | | | | | | | |
| Gold | | | | | | | | |
| Other Commodities | | | | | | | | |
| US Real Estate | | | | | | | | |
| Euro Real Estate | | | | | | | | |
| Asian Real Estate | | | | | | | | |

# A Brief Asset Class Review-Gold

At GaveKal, we have the tremendous privilege of talking regularly to extremely bright clients, located all over the world and who look at very different parts of the markets. We do not mention this to brag but to underline that the diversity of our client base is undeniably the greatest asset of our research product. Through constant communications with our clients (we do spend a fair amount of time on the road), we not only gain exposure to great new ideas, but we also enjoy massive "push-back" when our ideas are stupid. Very often, we are invited to review our assumptions, and conclusions, by clients whose experience, knowledge of the markets, and wits are usually far greater than our own. We are very lucky in that our clients are typically very generous with their feedback (especially when we are wrong).

Why do bring this up? Because when we discuss the issues reviewed in the above chapters, most of our clients conclude that the most likely "heads I win, tails I don't lose" investment in the world that we describe could very well be gold. After all, they tell us:

- If the central banks continue to manipulate their currencies, they will end up with excess reserves. Some of these reserves will flow into gold and gold prices will move higher…

- If the US economy implodes, the Fed will be tempted to slash interest rates and dump money into the system, which would be highly favorable to gold.

- If a European debt crisis does flare up, European investors will be scared and run into gold, while the Asian central banks who have been buying European bonds will also seek shelter in the barbarous relic.

These points are, of course, very valid. And could well turn out to be true. But try as we may, we have a really hard time getting excited about gold, especially at current levels when it is trading much above its marginal cost of production (probably around US$350/oz?).

Our biggest problem with holding gold as a hedge against the system we currently live in imploding, is that, at the end of the day, gold is a negative cash flow asset. In other words, when you put money in gold, it just sits there and provides no return whatsoever (in fact, it costs a little to store). The main attraction with gold is the premise that, down the road, someone who was not smart enough to buy the precious metal today, will buy it back from you at a higher price.

Now, undeniably, in the financial markets one often finds periods where buying negative cash flow assets to sell them back to some greater fool a few months (or years) later at a higher price has paid off handsomely. For example, people who bought negative cash flow dot-com companies in 1998 and sold them back in early 2000 into an eager market made out like bandits. But finding the "greater fool" who will buy back your negative cash flow asset is much easier in an ample liquidity environment and stable and fluid markets. At times of financial dislocations, anything can happen. And one of the things that often happens is that negative cash flow assets, all of a sudden, find no buyers.

In essence, negative cash flow assets live on borrowed time, or borrowed money. And when the latter runs out (say, for example, if a Europe faces a debt crisis, or if the US economy hits the wall, or if Asia stops exporting large amounts of capital), the former usually runs out as well.

Today, investors are again happy to pile into negative cash flow assets such as gold and silver, on the premise that these metal bars will be easily sold at a higher price to an ETF, or to an Asian central bank, or to Middle Eastern investors eager for more gold, or to the growing number of Indians getting married. But is this as safe a trade as people believe it is?

The fact that gold is by its very nature a negative cash flow asset probably helps explain why gold has always done poorly when the yield curve was flat or inverted (see chart).

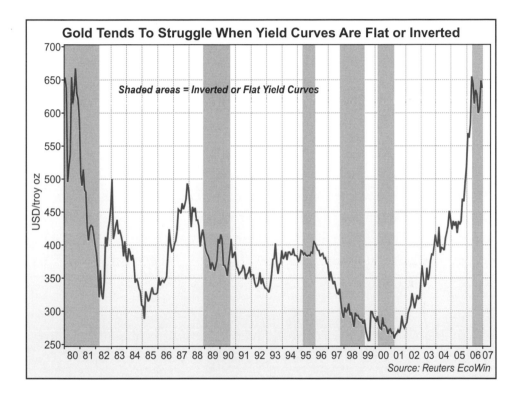

Having said that, the common perception remains that gold is "a store of value" for the simple reason that gold has been the one asset which government could not really manipulate, or destroy. Of course, in the past twenty years, investors have been offered an ever growing array of financial tools with which to hedge the risk of government manipulation: T-Bond futures, Tips, an ever growing range of derivative products... But these products are only on offer to Western investors. Meanwhile, a growing part of global economic growth is taking place outside the western World; in countries such as China and India. And these countries consequently have an ever growing number of individuals with disposable savings to protect from the rapacious tentacles of the government. Now, as things stand, the poor Chinese or Indian rentiers have few tools at their disposal to hedge the devious schemes their respective governments might put in place to spoil them. Local investors in most now-Western world countries simply do not have the tools at their disposal to diversify their portfolios away from their local currencies.

As countries like China and India get richer, it is thus easy to make a case for a continued rise in the demand for gold. But one has to remember that this demand could prove highly unstable. If, one day, Indian and Chinese individuals are allowed to diversify away from domestic assets, then not only will the demand for gold collapse, but a new supply will be "dug out of the back garden" by investors wanting to diversify into US equities, EMU bonds etc…One day very soon (see the recent noises about making the Rupee a convertible currency, or allowing some of China's US$1.4tr in private savings to be invested abroad through QDII schemes), India and China will lift their exchange controls. And, on that day, gold will find no bids; just offers. The lifting of exchange controls in India or China is a Damocles sword hanging over gold's head.

Beyond our fear that, one day, this Damocles sword will fall right on top of the gold investors' heads, we must also admit that we have a "philosophical" aversion to investing in the yellow metal. Indeed, a currency usually has to offer some of the following attributes:

- A mean of exchange

- A standard of value

- A reserve of value

- Through interest rates (administered at the short end by the central bank), a tool to collapse the future into the present and to value on the same date assets with different durations.

But does a currency need to offer all attributes? This is an important question which has divided economic thinkers for centuries. Indeed, going to the origins of our civilization, Aristotle explained that money had to have a value in itself; that it had to be desirable as a merchandise. And that gold and silver were thus by nature, the best form of money. Meanwhile, Plato thought money was, by its very nature, just a convention, necessary to facilitate transactions, but little else.

Strange as it may seems, this debate which is now more than two thousand years old, is still not settled. For example, today, Jim Grant (the extremely talented editor of *Grant's Interest Rate Observer*) or our good friend Marc Faber (the just as talented author of the *Gloom Boom Doom Report*) are openly and clearly disciples of Aristotle. Money, they frequently write in their reports, has to have an intrinsic value, otherwise, the risk is that it will inherently move to being worthless.

The problem, we believe, is that in today's world money has no intrinsic value (if for no other reason that it has practically no cost of production). We live in a Platonic world where money is a convention of a contractual nature. This has been the case since 1972 and the break-down of Bretton Woods. And this is why the gold bugs have been warning us that the current system is unsustainable for so long.

Aristotelians will tend to see current accounts as "profit and loss" statements, with the necessary transfers of gold to settle any deficits. Platonicians, like us, will meanwhile argue that deficits can simply be settled by selling assets (why would goods have to be exchanged for other goods? Why couldn't goods be exchanged for assets?) and that as long as asset prices rise as fast, or faster, than current account deficits, there is little to worry about.

Aristotelians will also tend to believe that central banks have no responsibility for economic growth; their sole responsibility is maintaining the value of the currency... In a sense, the last true experiences with Aristotelian central banking might have been the UK in the 1920s with the valiant defense of the Gold Standard by Winston Churchill (which nearly finished off the country economically). Or maybe Portugal under Salazar (Salazar was an economist who, with his belief in the gold standard, pushed Portugal into a hard-core depression even worse than the one currently imposed by the ECB). In the next slowdown, we will find out whether the ECB's board is Aristotelian or Platonic.

Finally, Aristotelians will argue that, if money does not have "value" in itself, over time, the government will just debase the value of the money and the average person will end up poorer. This, of course, sounds like a very logical claim, born out by experience. However, at the same time, one could argue that, while the average person might end up poorer because of government debasing, the average person is sure to end up much poorer under a gold standard system.

Our starting point is that, in order to trade, the world needs money. And for a "money" to be accepted by participants, it needs to present the first three characteristics presented above (mean of exchange, standard of value, reserve of value). And, of course, one could easily conclude that gold fits all three of the above criteria. Moreover, gold has the added advantage of not being prone to manipulation from governments.

However, we believe, gold is not a solution for a few simple reasons, which, incidentally, are the reasons gold systems broke down in the past. As we see it, the goals of any monetary system should be:

a)  To provide enough liquidity for the normal growth of international trade and economic activity to take place

b)  To offer a mechanism that allows for random shocks, (i.e.: oil price increases, financial crisis...) to be absorbed without too much pain.

The gold exchange standard and the dollar/gold exchange standard failed on both accounts for the following reasons:

- **Reason #1:** There is no reason to expect the physical discoveries of gold to be correlated to the expansion of world trade or economic activity. As such, in a gold system, we either face an overabundance in the means of payments (Europe after the discovery of Latin American gold), or a cruel lack of money (world trade in the 19th Century or in the 1930s). This unnatural over-supply/undersupply situation leads the global economy into completely unnecessary huge booms and busts (which is why the average person suffers more).

- **Reason #2:** Countries that accumulated large inventories of gold were usually very reluctant to move into a balance of payments deficit and allow those who had a problem to return to equilibrium. As a result, the system ran with a deflationary bias; the countries with a deficit were forced to move to a very restrictive policy because the ones with the surplus were neutral at best (which is also why the average person suffers more).

So between Aristotle and Plato, and as far as money is concerned, there is little doubt in our mind that Plato had the most foresight. Gold just doesn't work as a currency and is unlikely to ever be adopted again.

Leaving the Greeks behind and turning to what remains one of the most important economic texts ever written, namely the Scriptures (our French-speaking readers should pick up Charles' book *Un Liberal Nommé Jesus*) we find (in Matthew 25:14): *"For it is just like a man about to go on a journey, who called his own slaves and entrusted his possessions to them. To one he gave five talents, to another, two, and to another, one, each according to his own ability; and he went on his journey. Immediately the one who had received the five talents went and traded with them, and gained five more talents. In the same manner the one who had received the two talents gained two more.* But he who received the one talent went away, and dug a hole in the ground and hid his master's money.

*Now after a long time the master of those slaves came and settled accounts with them. The one who had received the five talents came up and brought five more talents, saying, "Master, you entrusted five talents to me. See, I have gained five more talents.' His master said to him, "Well done, good and faithful slave. You were faithful with a few things, I will put you in charge of many things; enter into the joy of your master.' Also the one who had received the two talents came up and said, "Master, you entrusted two talents to me. See, I have gained two more talents.' His master said to him, "Well done, good and faithful slave.... And the one also who had received the one talent came up and said, "Master, I knew you to be a hard man, reaping where you did not sow and gathering where you scattered no seed.* "And I was afraid, and went away and hid your talent in the ground. *See, you have what is yours.' But his master answered and said to him,* "You wicked, lazy slave, you knew that I reap where I did not sow and gather where I scattered no seed. *"Then you ought to have put my money in the bank, and on my arrival I would have received my money back with interest. "Therefore take away the talent from him, and give it to the one who has the ten talents.'*

*For to everyone who has, more shall be given, and he will have an abundance; but from the one who does not have, even what he does have shall be taken away. Throw out the worthless slave into the outer darkness; in that place there will be weeping and gnashing of teeth".*

Obviously, as far as Jesus-Christ is concerned, the notion that money is supposed to be a store of value doesn't carry much weight. For Christ, money is first and foremost a means of exchange; a tool to trade. The servant who simply aims to "preserve capital" is banished to the *"outer darkness, in that place where there will be weeping and gnashing of teeth"*.

And, as the chart below highlights, the "outer darkness" in the past century has, for all intents and purposes, been the gold market. Indeed, despite two or three world wars (whether one counts the cold war), a supposed massive debasement of our currencies (as the gold bugs like to say), hyper inflation, and the recent Gold rally, Gold has returned a princely-9% real in 111 years! We have also rarely seen four consecutive years of gains (1930s, early 1970s, late 1970s, 2002-2006). Meanwhile, the Dow Jones (without dividends re-invested!) has put in a far more honorable performance.

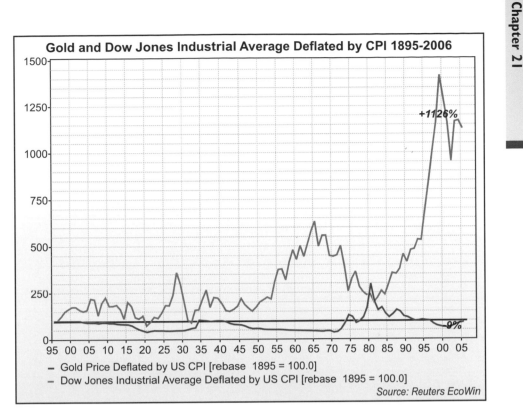

Christ was right. Money is first and foremost a tool of exchange. Money is not meant to stay idle doing nothing. And investing in gold is allowing for money to stay idle. Investing in gold is thus simply un-Christian. No wonder the Calvinists like it so much.

# A Longer Asset Class Review–Equities

Violent swings in markets usually happen at times of large divergences between the perception of reality and reality itself. Today, the perception of reality is that the US economy is on its way to the poor house through profligacy. The method of transport of the US economy to the poor house will either be a collapsing exchange rate, or, more likely, a collapsing stock market. In turn, the collapse in the US equities, will, as we are sometimes told, impact equity markets around the world.

But looking at US equity markets today (and, frankly, most equity markets around the World), we have a tough time understanding why we should not be overweight equities (we will make our case using US data because it is available and long dating, but the arguments we present below also work for the UK, Swiss, Japanese, Swedish, German… markets). Studying the last revision to third quarter US GDP, one thing is clear: the US profit machine just keeps on cranking. Year-over-year corporate profits (accounting for the inventory valuation adjustment and capital consumption allowance), surged 31.5%-and this happened as real GDP moderated to a 3% year-over-year pace! As we tried to show in chapter 9, and will show again now, the profitability of corporate America is truly stunning. Profit margins tower over anything we have seen in the post-War economy.

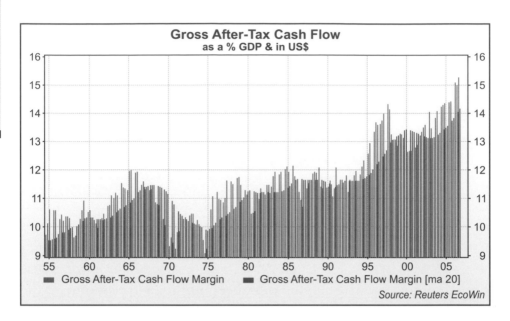

Of course, one could argue that these profits are "top of the cycle" profits and that profits are set to "return to the mean". Though, interestingly, the chart above demonstrates that, contrary to popular belief, margins have hardly been, in the past fifty years, a "mean reverting series". Instead, margins have moved from the lower left to the upper right; and, as our good friend Dennis Gartman would say, you want to own things that move from the lower left to the upper right!

So why have profit and cash flow margins been so strong? In chapter 9, we highlighted several explanations including the facts that:

- In most countries around the world, the size of the government in the economy has shrunk (look at the "upper left to lower right trend" in taxes as a % of profits). As the government takes less out of the pockets of shareholders, it means higher post-tax profits.

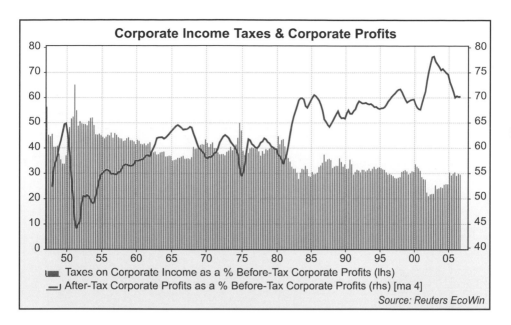

**Corporate Income Taxes & Corporate Profits**

Taxes on Corporate Income as a % Before-Tax Corporate Profits (lhs)
After-Tax Corporate Profits as a % Before-Tax Corporate Profits (rhs) [ma 4]

*Source: Reuters EcoWin*

• The collapse of inflation has helped margins tremendously. Instead of being saddled with monster borrowing bills, companies can now borrow and deploy capital without having to worry that the borrowing costs will cripple their future profits.

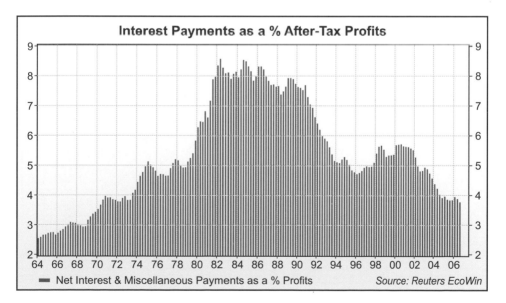

**Interest Payments as a % After-Tax Profits**

Net Interest & Miscellaneous Payments as a % Profits

*Source: Reuters EcoWin*

- Companies in the western world are increasingly outsourcing all activities in which they have a low, or negative, return on invested capital and focusing on their core competencies. As David Ricardo handsomely proved, free trade works to everyone's benefit.

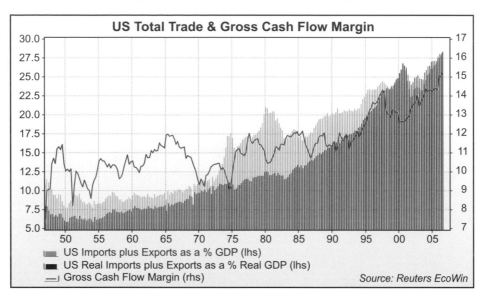

Finally, and probably most importantly, western economies are transforming themselves from an industrial economy to a "knowledge-based' economy.

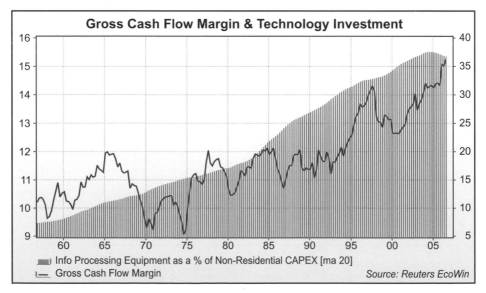

In fact, we believe that there is logic to the idea that the western economies have become so dominated by trade and finance activities that profits data will not give us a clear perspective on the average domestic operation. The complexity of the overall aggregate data is becoming every day more mind-boggling.

Luckily, the BEA produces data on Non-Financial Domestic Corporate Business, which pertains to domestic companies engaged in activities other than finance and trade. The BEA doesn't provide us with revenues, costs and the residual that is profits; instead they give us "value added". The BEA defines this term as *"The portion of goods and services sold or added to inventory or fixed investment by a firm that reflects the production of the firm itself. It represents the firm's contribution to a country's gross domestic product, which is the value of goods and services produced by labor and property located in the country. Compared to sales, value added is a preferable measure of production because it indicates the extent to which a firm's sales result from their own production rather than from production that originates elsewhere."*

In other words, what value added tells us is the amount of knowledge US companies might add to a mix of raw ingredients. Dell, for example, may import a variety of parts: chips, drives, motherboards- and then assemble those parts into a final product. Value added tells us how much knowledge they infused in the process. A bucket of parts has X value, but those parts assembled into something of actual use has Y value. This is what "value added" captures.

It should follow then that, as the US economy has been transforming from an industrial economy to a knowledge economy, the value the US adds should be rising. As an aside, this also provides a reality check on those who would claim that the US is a nation of burger-flippers, a nation whose citizens are engaged primarily in low value added endeavours. If indeed the US was "trading down" from higher value added jobs (like making automobiles) to lower ones (like washing them), we would expect to see such a shift in the data. In fact, we do not. Instead, we witness a steady march higher in the value added of the US economy.

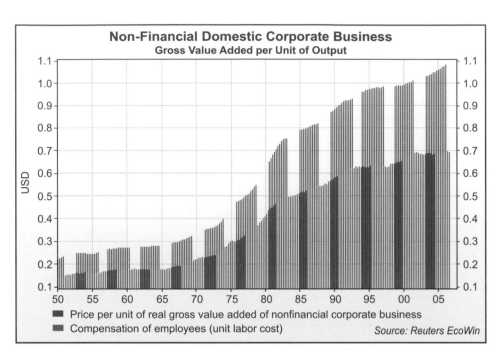

**Non-Financial Domestic Corporate Business**
Gross Value Added per Unit of Output

■ Price per unit of real gross value added of nonfinancial corporate business
■ Compensation of employees (unit labor cost)

*Source: Reuters EcoWin*

Along with a higher aggregate value added and value-per-unit created by employees, we would like to see the extent to which the corporate enterprise is adding value. Central to the definition of the platform company (presented in *Our Brave New World*) is the increase in value added by an enterprise (which optimizes the global supply chain and develops innovative new products)

So, we should expect, if our hypothesis of the nature and virtues of platform companies is correct, to see a rising level of value added by the corporate enterprise. Below is a chart of Non-Financial Domestic Corporate profits, before and after tax, per unit of output:

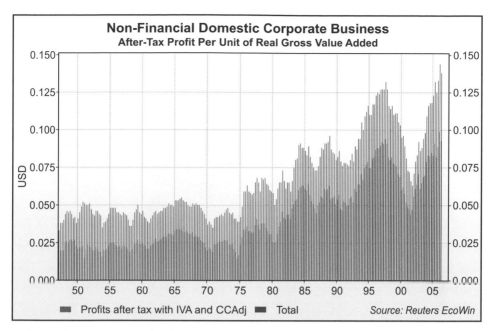

Taking this one step further, we can see the cash flow per unit of output that these companies are generating. Aggregate value added, profits and cash flow per unit of output went roughly sideways for the better part of 30 years after WW2, reflective of an industrial economy that produced

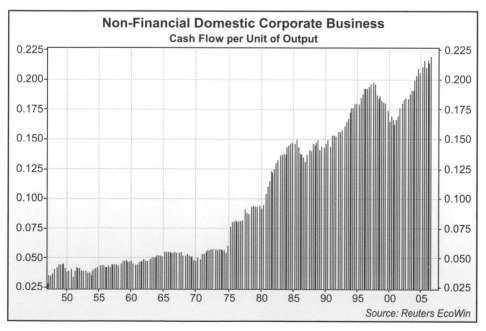

an ever greater amount of stuff but was not creating value. But then, starting in the 1980s, cash-flow per unit of output started to rise, and they have been soaring of late.

The US economy is no longer about producing "stuff"; it is about producing ideas. The infusion of knowledge into the goods and services the US produces is manifested in the rising value added in each unit produced. As our friend, Steve Waite, points out in his book _Quantum Investing:_ "_The weight of current economic output is modestly higher than it was a half a century ago even though its value is three times as great…Since 1977, government statisticians have measured the total weight of everything that goes into producing the value of goods each year. The annual tally of the weight of all raw materials, agricultural products, manufactured goods, and the like was 1.17 trillion pounds in 1977. By 2000, the weight of the US GDP had declined to 1.08 tn pounds. In the same period, the nominal dollar value of GDP doubled, from $4.3 tn to $8.6 tn._"

Companies own two types of assets: tangible assets and financial assets. Tangible assets are property, plant and equipment (the "heavy" capital intensive, cyclical stuff); financial assets items, things like cash, Treasury

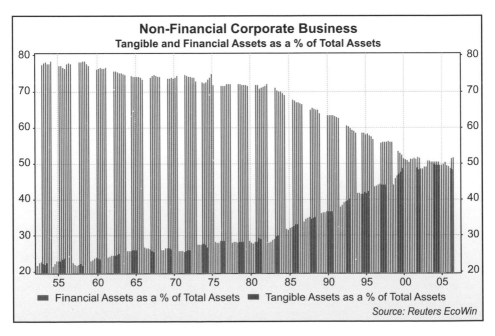

**Non-Financial Corporate Business**
Tangible and Financial Assets as a % of Total Assets

Financial Assets as a % of Total Assets ■ Tangible Assets as a % of Total Assets

_Source: Reuters EcoWin_

Bonds, trade receivables, etc. are the "lighter", more liquid, less risky assets. Now, interestingly, as the composition of the products produced in America has changed, so has the constitution of corporate America's balance sheet.

The chart above shows the composition of assets and how these have changed in recent years. The bottom line is simple: because the US produces ideas and adds value through infusing knowledge in the goods it produces, it requires less heavy assets. Indeed, if we compare the amount of financial assets-or those assets that are readily converted to cash-to the total amount of liabilities, we can see that corporate America is, today, a net creditor.

Of course, one is unlikely to read about America's amazing corporate health on the cover of *The Economist* or *The Financial Times* (though one did find it on the cover of *Barron's* on December 22nd, 2006) But, nevertheless, this is what the data is telling us.

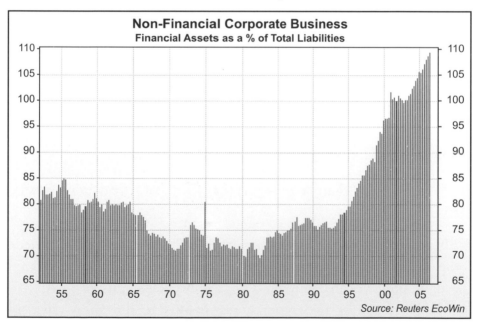

Let us next turn our attention to the actual amount of profits and cash produced by these non-financial enterprises. This next chart is the US$ value of these profits and cash flow.

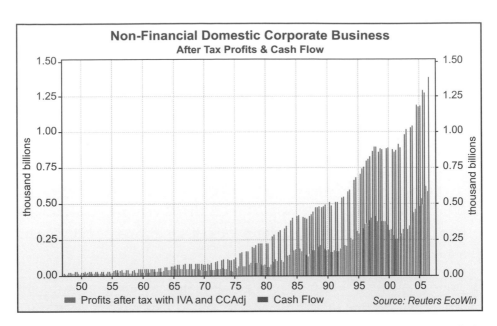

**Non-Financial Domestic Corporate Business**
After Tax Profits & Cash Flow

Profits after tax with IVA and CCAdj ■ Cash Flow    *Source: Reuters EcoWin*

Now that we have a pretty good fix on the sources of the profits and the size of the profits, let's consider the uses of those profits. There are really only four things that a company can do with its profits. It can:

1) Capital spend (note: Since R&D investment and investments in intangible capital in general take place within the income statement, these companies have already invested in knowledge).

2) Pay down debt.

3) Make an acquisition.

4) Return it to shareholders in the form of dividends or stock buybacks.

**With respect to capital spending,** we don't have perfect knowledge about the amount of non-residential fixed investment done by these companies-but we can deduce it. If we simply take the proportion of fixed capital consumed by these companies (relative to the total) and apply that percentage to aggregate capital expenditures, we can approximate the amount spent on Capex. What we see is that today US companies have positive free cash flow-to the tune of over US$100 billion.

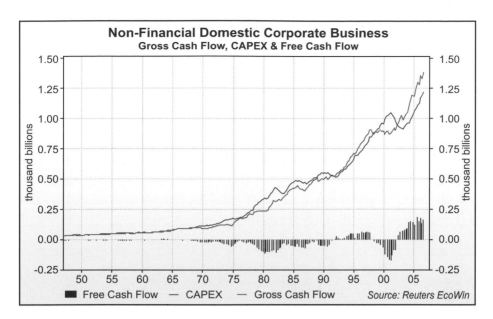

**Next on the list, companies can pay down debt.** Well, they've done that too.

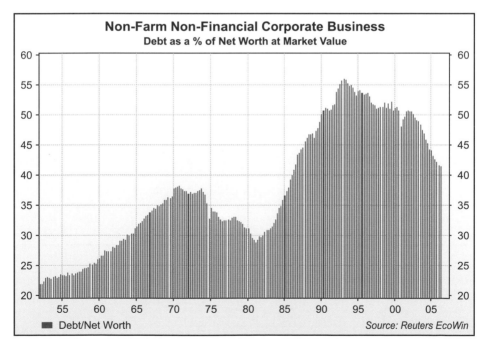

Since their business models are more stable (given the lack of capital intensity) and more profitable, we would expect debt levels not to fall to historic lows. In fact, we would expect managers to want to lever returns to an even greater extent than they appear to be doing today.

**There is no way to quantify the extent of a company's desire to make an acquisition,** so we can't analyze that one. Suffice it say that, with all the recent deal activity, the urge to merge seems quite high right now.

**Last on our list—and this is the most exciting part—is the distribution of capital to shareholders.** This can be done either through the payment of a dividend or the repurchase of stock. Non-Financial companies have lately been using both avenues quite generously.

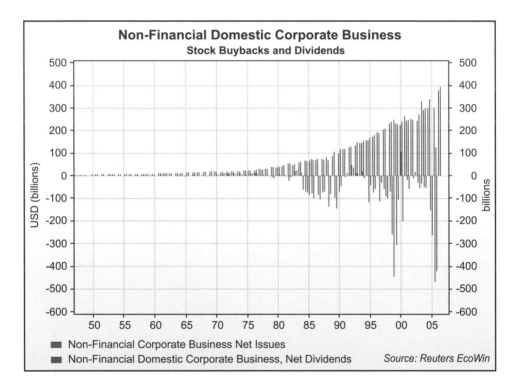

**Non-Financial Domestic Corporate Business**
Stock Buybacks and Dividends

■ Non-Financial Corporate Business Net Issues
■ Non-Financial Domestic Corporate Business, Net Dividends    *Source: Reuters EcoWin*

Combining buyback and dividends, we end up with the aggregate amount of capital that companies are distributing to shareholder—and that sum is today approaching US$1 trillion!

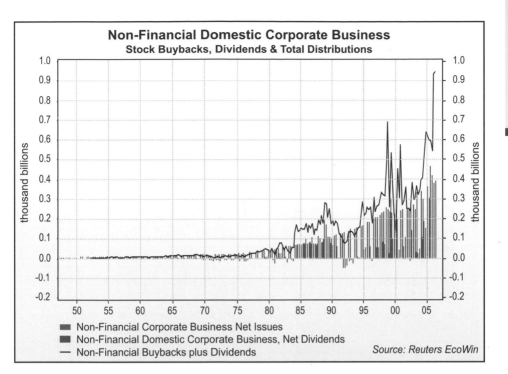

**Non-Financial Domestic Corporate Business**
Stock Buybacks, Dividends & Total Distributions

- Non-Financial Corporate Business Net Issues
- Non-Financial Domestic Corporate Business, Net Dividends
- Non-Financial Buybacks plus Dividends

Source: Reuters EcoWin

We can then compare the total distributions to the market value of these firms, in order to arrive at a current yield. That figure is near 9% at present.

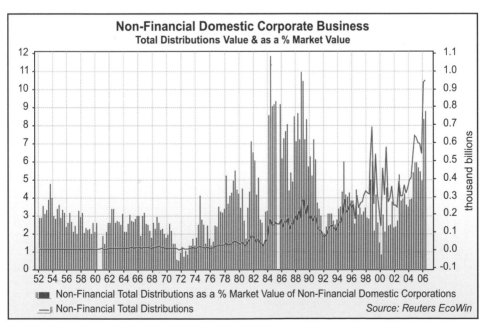

**Non-Financial Domestic Corporate Business**
Total Distributions Value & as a % Market Value

- Non-Financial Total Distributions as a % Market Value of Non-Financial Domestic Corporations
- Non-Financial Total Distributions

Source: Reuters EcoWin

For comparison sake, the earnings yield and cash flow yield are roughly 5% and 12% respectively.

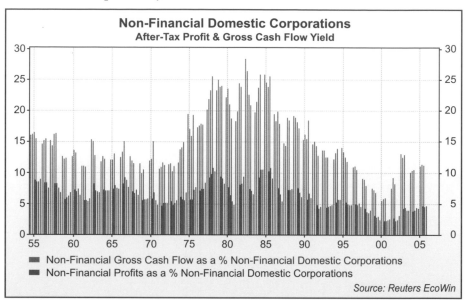

That means we have a situation where the non-financial domestic corporate earnings yield is below the current yield. This is simply amazing: Companies are paying out more money than they are earning. How long can that last?

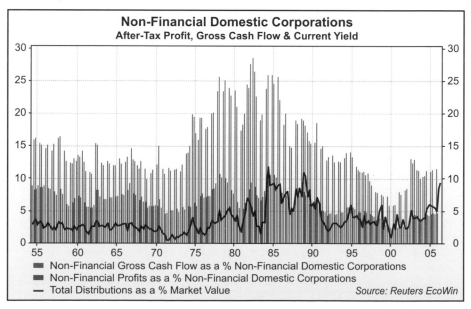

We have spent a lot of energy in recent years arguing that we need to re-consider some of our assumptions about the way companies work and the way wealth is created in "*Our Brave New World*". We would like now to introduce what seems to us a self-evident truth: the nature of the assets on the US corporations' balance sheet has changed dramatically in the past twenty years. Simply put, balance sheets are no longer full of heavy, capital-intensive assets which are consumed in the generation of revenues and earnings. In fact, increasingly, companies seem to be holding assets that increase in value, generate a passive income, or a capital gain.

This is very important since earnings are the product of a stock of productive (physical) assets, while passive income or capital gains do not flow through the income statement. In other words, the more financial assets or appreciating tangible assets a company owns, the more wealth the company creates outside of its income statement.

It used to be that corporate wealth creation was solely the function of profits. But today, companies are creating wealth in new ways, outside of the income statement. We need to evaluate this wealth creation in order to arrive at a deeper understanding of whether the current pay-outs by US companies are sustainable. This is what we do in the following pages and conclude that these "alternative sources of wealth" are what is being monetized today to allow for the record level of capital distribution. We also conclude that these record levels of distribution can go on for a long while still. **When looking at companies, we need to think beyond profit margins and in ever broader terms when considering the wealth creation capabilities of managements.**

In *Our Brave New World*, we argued that companies in the Western World would start to feel that outside shareholders were increasingly a hassle and would thus start to get rid of them. And sure enough, in recent years, companies in the US and around the OECD have been withdrawing capital from the markets at an unprecedented pace. Last year, on a market capitalization of around $11 trillion, non-financial US companies reduced their float by around 5%!

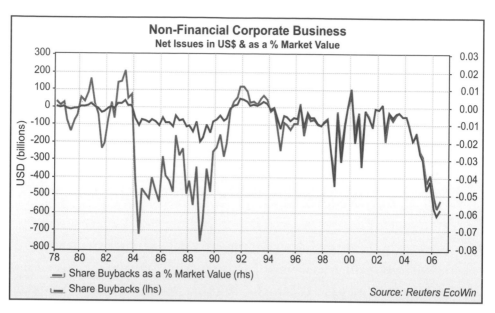

Only in the mid 1980s-the golden age of LBO, *Barbarians at the Gate* and all that-were shares reduced faster as a percentage of market value. At the time, this was simply a cost of capital arbitrage: inflation plunged, real interest rates fell, and debt was exchanged for equity.

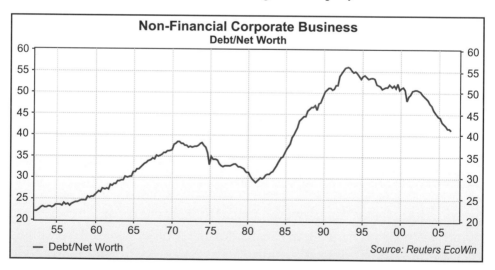

But this time, things are clearly different: debt is falling and shares are declining. As a result, corporate net worth is surging: And this is not due to de-capitalization, since capital expenditures stand today above depreciation. We are thus witnessing net additions to the US capital stock.

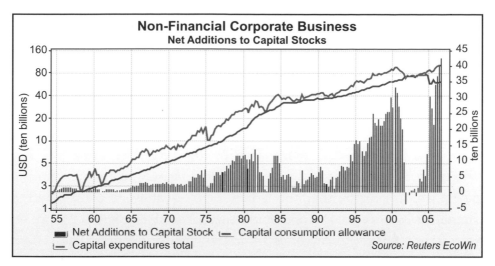

Putting it all together in the US (and across the OECD) today:

a) Companies are paying out more money than they are earning,

b) Companies are adding to their capital stock,

c) Companies are buying back stock and

d) Companies are reducing leverage on their balance sheet.

But how is this not mutually exclusive?

The answer is, we believe, simple: a growing number of US companies (and companies around the world) are adopting the "platform company" business model. And, in turn, this changes the way we should look at and analyse them.

As a company adopts the "platform company" business model, the mixture of assets on the balance sheet changes. Typically, balance sheets are no longer bogged down with heavy assets, like machinery, that depreciate, are illiquid and generate low returns within the income statement. Instead, balance sheets are now full of lighter, more liquid, sometimes appreciating assets. These assets can create wealth inside and outside of the income statement. At the same time, as a company adopts the "platform company" model, it tends to become more efficient with its working capital (think of Wal-Mart or Carrefour's treasury operations) and monetizes this efficiency.

As reviewed just above, as the US economy moved from an industrial economy to a knowledge-based service economy, the stock of assets changed (from 75% fixed and 25% liquid to 50%-50%). We further suspect that the mix of tangible assets has changed as well. Unfortunately, we do not have the data breakdown to illustrate this, but given that 90% of the US workforce is now employed outside of manufacturing, maybe we can assume that about 10% of the real estate owned by US companies is industrial? This would mean that 90% of US corporate real estate is made up of office buildings, malls and other, i.e.: more valuable and more liquid real estate. After all, how many buyers are there for shuttered multi-acre industrial parks in Flint, Michigan? As far as we know, pension funds and investors aren't lining up to bid on these properties. Meanwhile, cap rates on office buildings in New York City or San Francisco are below fed funds and hedge funds are clamoring for companies like McDonald's to unlock value from their real estate holdings…The bottom line is simple: the current real estate holdings of corporate America (which constitutes 30% of total assets) has most likely been appreciating at a healthy clip in recent years, thereby creating wealth for shareholders.

Below is a picture of how much wealth. Holding gains on real estate (the passive appreciation of the property) have been roughly US$800 billion per annum for each of the past few years. That's US$800 billion that doesn't flow through the income statement. Undeniably, corporate America has participated in the real estate boom of the last few years…and is well positioned to continue participating should the boom continue.

## Non-Financial Corporate Business
### Holding Gain on Real Estate

— Annualized Holding Gain on Real Estate    Source: Reuters EcoWin

As an aside, this is yet another reason we love government presentation of financial statements. The Fed, in its quarterly flow of funds, is kind enough to mark to market company assets. Under GAAP, assets are carried at historic cost or, in the case of tangible assets like property, depreciated historic cost. So, with GAAP, we have no way to see the wealth which flows through to shareholders from the appreciation of assets. With the Fed flow of funds, we do. This may seem trivial, but this is an important distinction: we increasingly need to view the balance sheet of companies as a multi-faceted source of wealth creation. This isn't to say that real estate prices will go up forever and that there will be constant capital gains to monetize, but we need to realize that the rise in real estate has been a source of wealth that has contributed to the reduction in shares outstanding (and thus stronger EPS).

Another source of wealth creation that falls outside the income statement is income from foreign direct investment. At US$2.2 trillion, foreign direct investment is the single largest (identified) financial asset held by non-financial US companies. US companies like Wal-Mart or Motorola have deployed huge sums of capital overseas in an effort to open new markets for their products, or processes.

Here is a chart of the annual flow of this investment, and the value of the stock.

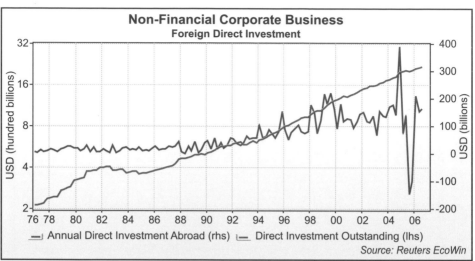

This next chart depicts the rise in foreign direct investment as a proportion of total assets; notice the surge which started in the late 1980s.

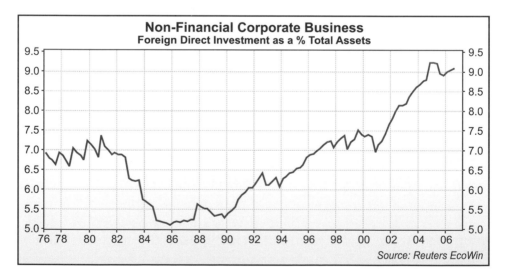

So if the earnings derived from foreign direct investment do not flow into corporate profits data, then where do we see them? And how big are they? The profits of US corporations captured outside of the US (i.e.:

the sale of a Dell laptop to GaveKal in Hong Kong) are captured, in the flow of funds report, in an account called "Foreign Earnings Retained Abroad". In 2006, they will reach around US$120bn.

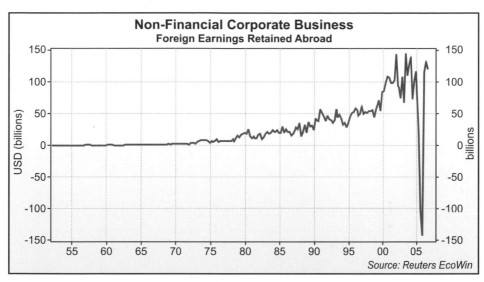

The spike down in 2005 coincided with a change in the tax law which allowed for a temporary tax reduction if these earnings were repatriated. However, aside from that 2005 tax event, US corporate profits abroad have been steadily growing and represent a meaningful percentage of

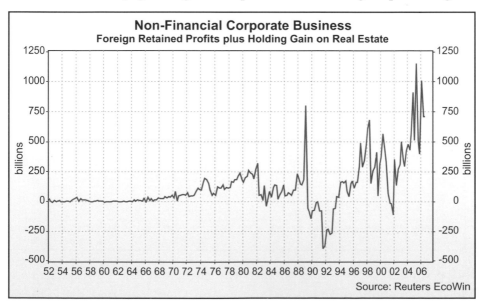

"inside the lines" earnings (earnings captured on the income statement in corporate profits data). Combining the holding gains on real estate and foreign retained profits, we come up with the following chart. Passive income and capital gains combined represented about 50% of stated corporate profits after tax last year.

Working capital improvements are another place where corporate America has unlocked value, monetized productivity gains and added another element of stability to its balance sheet. In the chart below, we can see (for US non-financial companies) the current ratio that relates liquid current assets to current liabilities. This improvement is largely a function of:

a) Inventory management improvements (with the employ of PCs, fiber-optic networks, RFID tags, GPS systems, software algorithms…) and

b) The fact that a growing number of platform companies pressure suppliers for better payment terms (try being a Wal-Mart supplier and see if you like it).

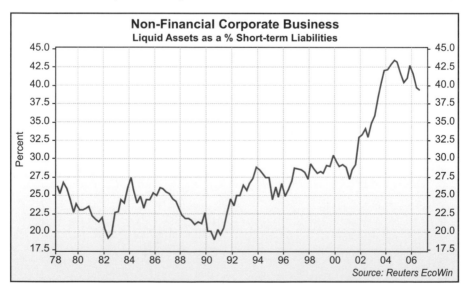

Non-Financial Corporate Business
Liquid Assets as a % Short-term Liabilities
Source: Reuters EcoWin

Today, the inventory stocks of American companies are no longer sitting idle on a manufacturing floor, warehouse shelf, or retail stock room.

They are in motion, on the back of ships, trains, trucks and planes. This has drastically improved the velocity of American business and reduced the amount of capital companies need to allocate to the delivery of a given product or service.

Below is a picture of inventory turnover for non-financial companies. We simply compare the gross value added of non-financial companies to the amount of inventory held on balance sheets. Undeniably, the velocity of business has accelerated dramatically over the last couple of decades.

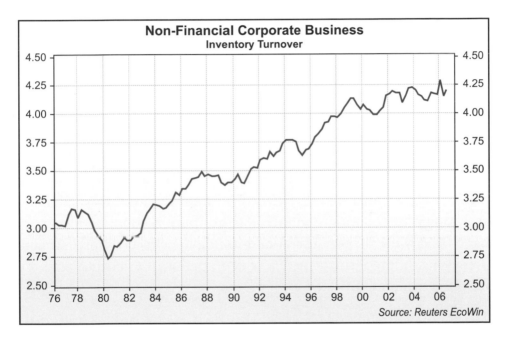

And the amount of capital required to finance working capital needs has plummeted (a possible explanation for the "excess capital" situation so many of the bears bemoan?).

In the chart below, net working capital is inventories plus accounts receivable, minus accounts payable. Total capital is the long-term proportion of credit market debt outstanding, plus all miscellaneous debt, plus the market value of equities outstanding. Whereas working capital consumed 30% of a company's total capital as recently as 30 years ago, it consumes only 10% today.

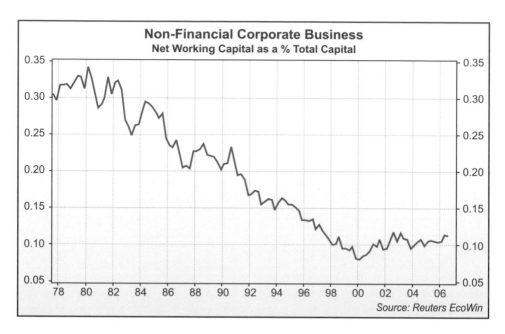

When we refer to US corporate profits, we (like most people) use after-tax profits adjusted for IVA and CCA. Now, both the inventory valuation and capital consumption adjustments are pure accounting sleight of hand. And while they are useful in distilling the effects of inflation and presenting a more accurate picture of depreciation, they are just made up numbers that are subtracted from profits.

The more interesting question is: what does a company really end up with? And the answer, we have always felt, is simple enough: cash flow. Cash flows are after-tax profits plus depreciation. And, taking this a step further, if we forget about accounting fiction, and focus on what ends up in the pockets of companies, we have some more adjustments to make. We need to add back the IVA and CCA (since these are non-cash charges); and what we end up with is a number that represents the total internally generated cash flow. And, at the end of the day, companies end up with the red line in their pocket (after paying the accountants to adjust down their profits). Not the grey line.

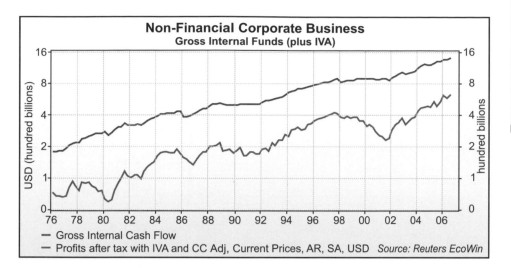

**Non-Financial Corporate Business**
Gross Internal Funds (plus IVA)

— Gross Internal Cash Flow
— Profits after tax with IVA and CC Adj, Current Prices, AR, SA, USD   *Source: Reuters EcoWin*

As the chart above illustrates, the wealth created "outside the lines" exceeds the wealth created "inside the lines". And, interestingly, this has been a fairly constant historic relationship. From here, companies have a variety of decisions to make:

a) How much should they spend on CapEx?

b) How much should they pay in dividends?

c) Should they borrow against unrealized wealth increases?

d) Should they buyback stock?

e) Should they pay down debt?

Or why not do it all? Out of $2,288.1 billion in wealth generated by US companies last quarter (on an annualized basis), US$1,030.3bn was spent on CapEx. This left $1,257.8 billion, of which $390.4 billion was cash. Companies then borrowed $932.5 billion and so had $1,322.9 billion in cash to throw around. They paid $395.9 billion in dividends and bought back $579.6 billion in stock for a total of $975.5 billion returned to shareholders (our current yield calculation). This still left corporations with $347.4 billion in cash and $866.6 in unrealized capital gains.

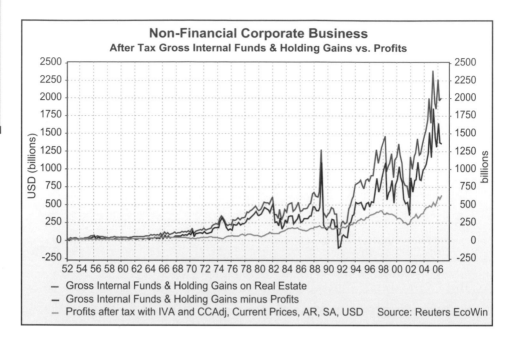

**Non-Financial Corporate Business**
After Tax Gross Internal Funds & Holding Gains vs. Profits

— Gross Internal Funds & Holding Gains on Real Estate
— Gross Internal Funds & Holding Gains minus Profits
— Profits after tax with IVA and CCAdj, Current Prices, AR, SA, USD    Source: Reuters EcoWin

Is this sustainable? It is long as companies continue to generate increases in wealth outside the income statement and are accommodated by the capital markets in monetizing these gains. But what if real estate stops rising (an important question these days)? Then companies can simply elect to stop buying back stock. So barring a real estate or a major financial accident (which would prevent companies from monetizing their gains), we find nothing harmful, unsustainable or otherwise precarious about the current situation.

The bottom line is simple enough: CEOs are compensated for the "inside the lines" per share wealth they generate. They are thus actively redirecting wealth created "outside the lines" back in. The fact that they can do so is a testament to the financial revolution our world is experiencing. Managers today have the ability to move, monetize and distribute wealth emanating from multiple sources of wealth creation in any number of ways.

Companies today are not sacrificing future earnings power in order to repurchase stock. Quite the reverse: companies are enhancing future earnings power–with capital additions- and levering the future returns that capital will generate. Companies are levering themselves to volume increases with working and fixed capital improvements. This is not a one-time effect: a lighter balance sheet and efficient working capital management is the gift that keeps on giving, since it will show up in future per share results. Companies have been able to increase their capital base, pay a dividend, buy back stock and have a falling debt to net worth ratio. To do this, they did not monetize reductions to their capital base; rather, they monetized increases in their wealth generated outside the bounds of the income statement.

This is all, we believe, very exciting. And, of course, it begs the question of what, we, as investors, must pay to get a piece of that great story. Amazingly, the answer is: very little. Indeed, when we compare the current yield to bond yields we find that we see we are getting paid 3% more to own non-financial US companies than we are to own US 10-year bonds (this dichotomy between bond yields and earnings yield is visible in numerous countries, including Japan, Sweden, France…).

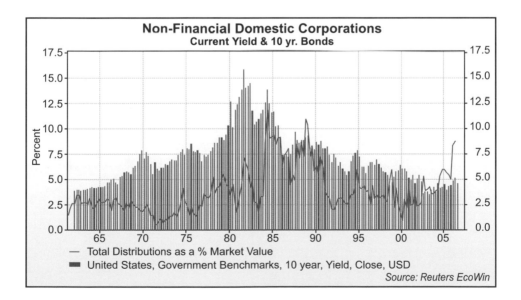

In addition, Non-Financial Corporate Businesses are also selling below book-value.

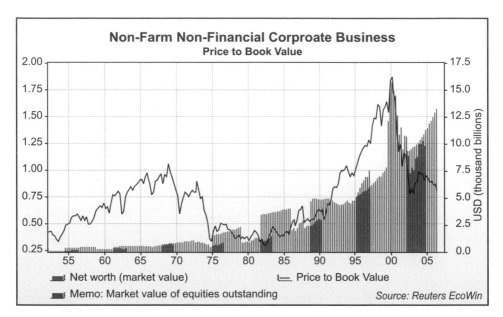

When looked at on a Free Cash Flow basis, US companies yield around 2% at present, or close to record highs.

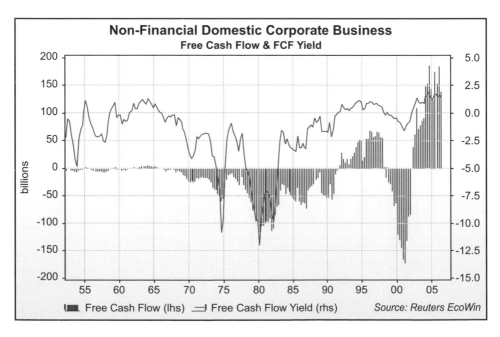

The fact of the matter is that producing ideas is wildly profitable and doesn't require a lot of capital. Each year, as the US economy becomes more and more of a knowledge-centric economy, companies realize they are overcapitalized and decide to lavish that excess capital on shareholders—unless private equity firms get their hands on it first.

So putting it all together, US profit margins are at record highs, the value added of the US economy—a reflection of the successful transformation into a knowledge economy—is at a record level, corporate debt levels are low, balance sheets are very light and very liquid; stock buyback and dividends are plentiful...and valuations languish.

How does this add up?

At the end of the day, an equity is a stream of future earnings, discounted by an interest rate, on which investors tack on a risk premium. Now, as we tried to show, we strongly believe that the stream of current strong earnings will prove to be highly sustainable. We also believe that, thanks to the fall in the volatility of global economic growth, risk premiums should come down (they have not, far from it). So barring a massive increase in interest rates, we have a hard time seeing why we should not remain (wildly) bullish on US and global equities. It feels like stealing.

# A Shorter Asset Class Review– Commodities

When we sit down with clients, and express our long term bullish views on global economic activity, our enthusiasm about equities, our hopes for Chinese and Asian growth (the subject of a soon to be published book) we usually get the same answer: "Hold on: you're telling me that global growth in 2007 will remain decent, that Asia will have a massive infrastructure boom, that Chinese real estate is going to go gangbusters and yet, at the same time, you tell me that I should not own commodities? This just doesn't add up".

This is a question to which we have a well-rehearsed answer: "Imagine that we are in 1946 and we describe to you a world of air-conditioners, neon

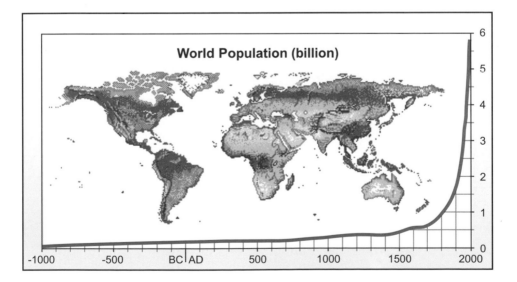

lights, electrical appliances, computers, jet airplanes, pleasure yachts, three car garages and the SUVs that go in them...Imagine we also show you how the world will grow from a total population of 1.5bn people to 6.5bn people... Imagine then that, in our great foresight, we saw how central banks would lose the plots, allow monetary aggregates to explode, move everyone to fiat-money, etc...Then we would have probably agreed that the best thing to own would have been commodities. In fact, we probably would have wanted to own nothing but commodities!"

And, of course, adjusted for inflation, commodities would have been one of the worst investments we could have made. Indeed, despite a boom in growth, the CRB index adjusted for inflation (see chart below) has had dismal returns.

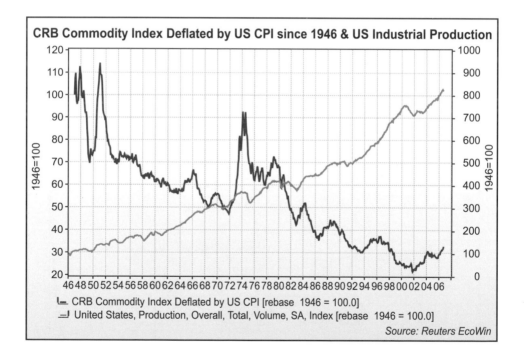

**CRB Commodity Index Deflated by US CPI since 1946 & US Industrial Production**

L— CRB Commodity Index Deflated by US CPI [rebase 1946 = 100.0]
—J United States, Production, Overall, Total, Volume, SA, Index [rebase 1946 = 100.0]

Source: Reuters EcoWin

So why, despite the great fundamental environment, did commodities fare so poorly? And what should we expect now that the growth rate of the global population is slowing, and even shrinking in most of the world's richer countries (Japan, Germany, Italy, Russia...)

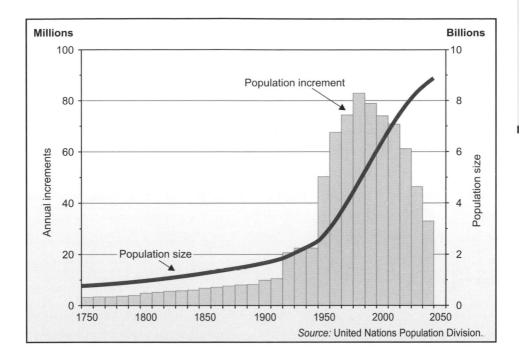

Source: United Nations Population Division.

The answer is, we believe, that commodities over the long-term tend to return to their marginal cost of production. And that thanks to technology, freer trade, lack of full-scale wars, etc…the marginal cost of production of almost all commodities has spent the past fifty years falling.

Which leaves us with an important question: today, commodity prices stand far above their cost of production (allowing producers to capture an inordinate rent); can this last? Commodity bears (like us) argue that it can't, that it never has in the past, and that it won't start now. Commodity bulls (like many of our clients) argue that, this time, and contrary to History, the marginal cost of production will rise substantially because of qualified labour shortages, supply constraints, environmental laws, etc…

At this juncture, the answers to this debate are extremely important. If the commodity bulls are right, and commodity prices continue to rise in the face of historical precedent, then it is likely that we will see a re-arranging of global geo-political power and a much lower growth rate around the world then what we expect (if for no other reason that higher commodity prices take money from the private sector to put it into public sector hands–for example, higher oil prices means less money in our pockets and more in the coffers of Hugo Chavez, Vladimir Putin, the Saudi royal family…). The bullish argument we presented above for equities could be undermined. If we are right and if commodities do return towards their marginal cost of production (and, at the end of the day, there is really only one commodity that truly impacts global activity: oil), then growth will likely be given a massive boost as money stops being transferred to public entities that waste it on projects such as financing Hizbullah, financing Castro, financing an Iranian nuclear bomb…

As an aside, we have to say that we admire our clients who, in regards to commodities, have the courage to bet against all historical precedents. We admire them not only because they made a lot of money in commodities in recent years (and we did not), but because they have the guts to stand up and say "this time it's different". Having uttered these words many times in recent years, and been laughed out of the room, we know that coming to such a conclusion takes, if nothing else, great courage.

# In Conclusion

There is no doubt in our minds that we live in a rapidly changing world. By preventing a market price (exchange rates) from adjusting to new economic realities, Asian central banks are undeniably creating ripples, and distortions, throughout the financial market. But will those distortions end in 2007? Perhaps they will… though, as we tried to show, the odds are that they won't. More importantly, the odds might be that the cracks in the system will not appear where most investors already expect them (i.e.: in the US$ and US equities) but perhaps appear elsewhere (Europe?). In any event, we doubt that 2007 will be the year when the world economy finally faces its "Day of Reckoning".

Ever since the start of the late 20th Century's great global expansion, many politicians, economists, and media commentators have been issuing dire warnings about the economic retribution which surely lies ahead after so many years of overindulgence in consumption, speculation and borrowing.

But there are many reasons for doubting such prophecies of doom—not least the strong probability that the US will actually avoid a recession and the dollar will soon rebound. But more interesting than such short-term forecasts are two observations about long-term economic trends.

The first is that the Prophets of Doom have predicted their day of reckoning, like Jehovah's Witnesses, at the beginning of almost every year since the mid- 1980s. And every time their predictions have turned out to be wrong, they have merely redoubled their warnings about the terrifying instability of the world economy. Instead of accepting that this argument had been refuted, they have insisted that financial or political manipulations have simply held off the collapse, thereby guaranteeing an even more wrathful Dies Irae when the reckoning finally arrives.

In arguing that postponing economic problems automatically magnifies these dangers, the Jehovah's Witness economists have misunderstood the most important virtue of a liberal, competitive economy–the fact it automatically encourages billions of intelligent, motivated and creative individuals to seek out solutions to whatever economic challenges the world may present. **In a competitive global economy, therefore, time is on the side of stability, not against it.** If governments refrain from tackling potential problems, in the way in which America, for example, has refrained from tackling the "unsustainable" trade deficits or Britain has refrained from tackling the "dangerous" level of mortgage borrowing, this does not automatically increase the potential danger. **In a liberal, competitive world, a problem postponed is not necessarily magnified.** On the contrary, a problem postponed is a problem well on the way to being solved.

Another, less philosophical, reason to ignore the Prophets of Doom has been their failure to understand the underlying forces which have powered the expansion of the global economy since the early 1990s. Specifically, there have been five: firstly, the collapse of communism, which has given three billion new consumers and producers the opportunity to enjoy the economic benefits of capitalism. Secondly, the spread of free trade, which has allowed these new capitalists to participate in the global economy for the first time. Thirdly, advances in electronic technology, which have cut communication costs almost to zero. Fourthly, a revolution in finance which has given consumers a freedom to manage both their assets and their borrowings, in a way that was once only possible for large multinational companies. Finally, the rediscovery of active demand management, which has allowed central banks to keep economies growing as close as possible to their long-run productive trends.

While some of these structural changes may seem to increase the risks in financial markets, their interaction has actually made the global economy more stable than ever before. For example, the shift of manufacturing employment from America to China has created huge trade imbalances. But the same globalisation process has made global trade imbalances easier to finance, and the shift from manufacturing to services in the US and in other advanced economies has made them more stable than ever before. This greater stability, in turn, has reduced the risks of household borrowing; and the freedom of households to borrow has made consumption more stable in the face of economic shocks, such as the collapse of technology shares or the terrorist attacks of 9/11.

Economists (ourselves included) are still far from understanding the full implications of all these changes—or of weighing them up against new long-term dangers such as climate change, demographic decline and widening disparities of income. We can, however, say one thing for certain: this year, the Jehovah's Witness economists and the Calvinists will yet again be proved wrong.

The end is not nigh.